The Child Influencers

Restoring the Lost Art of Parenting

The Child Influencers

Restoring the Lost Art of Parenting

Dan Adams

Home Team Press
Cuyahoga Falls, Ohio

Dan Adams is a speaker for:
Home Team Seminars
2206 20th Street
Cuyahoga Falls, Ohio 44223

The Child Influencers: Restoring the Lost Art of Parenting

Published by Home Team Press
2206 20th Street, Cuyahoga Falls, Ohio 44223

Cover art by David Moses

Printed in the United States of America

Library of Congress Catalog Card Number: 90-81765

ISBN number: 0-9626349-0-5

2nd Printing

This book is dedicated to

Jennifer, Katie, and Emily.

One day, your mom and I

will say the best of our

days on earth were those

spent together with you.

Table of Contents

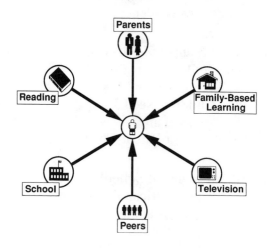

Acknowledgements

Have you ever heard the words, "You may enjoy your kids now, but just wait until they become teenagers!" For years my solace and silent rebuttal has been the family of Bill and Marcia Ihde. Carol and I have been inspired to see in their family the blessings that come when parents are the major influence in their children's lives. And throughout the writing of this book, Bill has been a wellspring of fresh ideas and resources. Bill, be it laid to your credit or your blame, you've provided the spark and kindling for this book and kept it well-stoked through completion.

Friends and family have given of themselves in many ways so that these ideas might reach the printed page. I want to thank... John and Edith Adams for 35 years of love and encouragement and lots of proofreading lately... Tom and Jean Balog (Carol's folks) for helping with the seminars and always looking for ways to support us... Joe and Gail Bujorian for their contribution of skillful editing... Dave Johnson for being our spiritual mentor and seminar "encourager"... John and Karen Lile for their kindred spirits and enduring support... David Moses for putting his heart as well as his brushes into the cover art... Paul Tell for his keen-but-kind editing eye, and... John and Cathy Wheaton for their deep friendship which led to untold evenings of contemplation, cover design, and Cookies-n-Cream ice cream.

Were it not for the brilliant life-work of certain men and women, you would now be reading the first pages of my *pamphlet* on parenting. Because I have immodestly chosen to write on a subject as broad as parenting, I have relied heavily on experts in specific areas such as discipline, reading, peer dependency, school, television, home education, etc. The contributions of some were so great that they cannot be left waiting patiently in the end-notes and bibliography. They are Karl Albrecht, Samuel Blumenfeld, Urie Bronfenbrenner, Paul Copperman, James Dobson, Mel and Norma Gabler, Victor and Mildred Goertzel, Gregg Harris, E. D. Hirsch, Jr., Tim LaHaye, Susan Schaeffer Macaulay, Jerry Mander, Raymond and Dorothy Moore, Neil Postman, Richard Restak, Phyllis Schlafly, Frank Stafford, Jim Trelease, John Whitehead, and Marie Winn.

My greatest appreciation goes to my wife and best friend, Carol. She *lives* the ideas in this book in a manner that makes writing of them a pleasure. All the more so because she helped so much in the writing effort. For without her sensitivity and editing skills, this book would be coarsely composed. Without her ideas, this book would be hollow. Without her love and encouragement, this book would be unwritten.

Dan Adams

Chapter 1

Introduction

June 17, 1943—A 20-year-old pilot starts the engine of his Westland Lysander on a runway in Sussex, England. At two o'clock in the morning, the sound of his engine pierces the lonely night. A single passenger climbs in and the plane rises heavily in the air. The aircraft, known as a moon plane, is painted a dull black, causing it to quickly disappear against the night sky. The pilot's destination: a quiet field near Le Mans in German-occupied France. His cargo: a striking young woman code-named Madeleine, destined to become the first woman radio-telegraph operator in the French underground resistance. By pale moonlight the pilot flies low over the English channel, then strains to see landmarks below. Finally, a prearranged pattern of lights on a deserted field comes into view, and he noses his plane down. In several minutes Madeleine will be making her way toward a railroad station, and he will be soaring back to England.[1]

Imagine yourself in the cockpit, peering into near-blackness. How would you feel about navigating in the dark, surrounded by danger, and responsible for precious cargo? If you are a parent, you may be on just such a mission! As you navigate your child toward adulthood, do you sense the many dangers surrounding you that have damaged so much other cargo? Do you peer into darkness that causes you to question your position and direction?

On that night in 1943, the pilot successfully completed his mission *because he was prepared.* He used three tools so well that he was able to repeat his performance over and over throughout the war... his maps, his flight instruments, and his flight training manual. For weeks he had been scrutinizing those maps, memorizing landmarks. He flew with the details of his course and destination burned into his mind. His flight instruments were the eyes that let him see that which he could not otherwise see—his altitude, his direction, his speed, his fuel supply. And his flight training manual was the most important of all. For without it, he would have never learned how to safely guide and land his craft.

This book is dedicated to introducing parents to the tools they need to navigate their important missions. We live in a day when many parents are not prepared to fly. Too often they become airborne, unsure of where they are headed, unable to measure their progress with reliable instruments, and un-trained to safely land their cargo. It need not be so.

Our Map—Historical Truth

A map is nothing more than the collected wisdom of those who have gone on before. It tells of landmarks we can use, warns us of dangers to avoid, and allows us to "see" our destination before we actually get there. It is crafted from the experience of those who have successfully returned from their journeys. Without a map, the navigator is reduced to the explorer, the experimenter, the gambler.

In post-World War II America, we have discarded our parenting maps, for the most part. We are now rearing our children in a fashion unlike that of any preceding generation. We are charting dangerous and unexplored territories, but since we don't look at the maps drawn by our forefathers, *we don't see the dangers until they are upon us.*

In this book we will return to past decades to understand how parenting was done. Just because something is "the way we used to do it," we won't assume it is the best way. But if it *worked*, we'd best pay attention to it. The thing about maps is that the bad ones usually get quickly thrown out. If you have a map that has been used over and over for a long time, though, you can probably count on its getting you to where you want to go.

Our Flight Instruments—Research Truth

Flight instruments tell you something you are going to find out anyway. But it's nice to know your fuel tank level *before* it's empty, and it helps to know your altitude is dropping while you are *still* in the air! The same is true with research on child-rearing. Through the study of large groups of children and parents, we can learn of the predictable outcome of our behavior. And it certainly helps to know these things *before* our children grow up.

In this book, we will examine a number of sources to glean research truth—government statistics, university studies, Congressional testimony, studies of the brain, and so on. The subjects of this research will be wide in scope, touching on aspects of child-rearing such as parent-child interaction time, TV-viewing, reading, day-care, peer dependency, tutoring, parent-child understanding, discipline, mental and social development, academic achievement, and creative play.

Like the pilot's flight instruments, this research is nothing more than a tool for measuring reality. And like those instruments, the research is not infallible. Yet, if we take the time to look at our instruments, and we understand how to read them, they can greatly help us navigate safely to our destination.

Our Flight Training Manual—Biblical Truth

I believe this to be the most important tool we have for completing our mission. A skilled airman has diligently studied each page of his flight training manual and applied the lessons during hundreds of hours of flight training. Only then can he operate his craft confidently, with each motion coming naturally to him. When the evening newspaper tells of a teenager who has wrecked his life just as it was beginning, I wonder, "Was this precious cargo taken aloft by unskilled hands that had not opened their training manual?"

Did you ever buy a Christmas toy that included the words, "Some Assembly Required"? Yet, even as you shuddered at those words, you knew the manufacturer had inserted at least a few cryptic pages of instructions inside the box to help you. When a child is born, there will be "assembly required" as that child's character develops. I believe The Manufacturer has included a complete set of instructions which we can find by opening the Bible.

If you believe the wisdom of the Bible is worth reading and applying to your life, you are in good company (Figure 1.1). Ultimately, though, the worth of the Bible does not come from without, but rather from within its covers, for it is the very Word of God:

> All scripture is God-breathed and is useful for teaching, rebuking, correcting and training in righteousness, so that the man of God may be thoroughly equipped for every good work.
>
> II Timothy 3:16[2]

It is impossible to rightly govern the world without God and
the Bible.
- George Washington

The Bible is no mere book, but a Living Creature, with a
power that conquers all that oppose it.
- Napoleon Bonaparte

The Bible is worth all other books which have ever been
printed.
- Patrick Henry

That book, sir, is the rock on which our republic rests.
- Andrew Jackson

I believe the Bible is the best gift God has ever given to
man. All the good from the Savior of the world is
communicated to us through this book.
- Abraham Lincoln

Hold fast to the Bible as the sheet-anchor of your liberties.
- Ulysses S. Grant

In all my perplexities and distresses, the Bible has never
failed to give me light and strength.
- Robert E. Lee

I have known ninety-five of the world's great men in my
time, and of these eighty-seven were followers of the Bible.
The Bible is stamped with a Specialty of Origin, and an
immeasurable distance separates it from all competitors.
- W. E. Gladstone

A man has deprived himself of the best there is in the world
who has deprived himself of this.
- Woodrow Wilson

Figure 1.1

When You Sit at Home...

For the first bit of wisdom from the Bible, let's look at
Deuteronomy 6:6,7:

> These commandments that I give you today are to be upon your
> hearts.
> Impress them on your children. Talk about them when you sit at
> home and when you walk along the road, when you lie down
> and when you get up.[3]

Now here is a radical thought: If we are interacting with
our children for less than a half-hour per day (as the studies
show), it will be hard to practice the above passage. In other
words, if we are not even *with* our children when we are sitting
at home, walking along the road, lying down, and getting up,
it's going to be hard to teach God's commandments at these
times.

This hasn't been an easy lesson for me to learn. Several
years ago, Jennifer asked her mommy why I was always
bringing work home in my briefcase. Carol explained that I
just couldn't get it all done during the day. Jennifer looked up
at her with those big blue eyes and asked, "Couldn't they put
him in a slower group?"

Well, maybe it didn't happen exactly like that. But the
point is, whatever "group" I'm in, my children *need* my time.
To see the effect absentee dads can have, imagine two scenes.
In the first, the family has no daddy. A little girl in that family
could run some serious risks. She could, for instance, crave
the male attention she lacks and have boy problems in her teen
years.

In the second scene, there is a daddy who comes home
each night. He immediately plops himself down in the Lazy
Boy (appropriately named), and begins reading the newspaper. Then it's "Supper, Honey," so he heads to the kitchen.

(We're giving him the benefit of the doubt here. After all, *somebody* is buying and using those TV trays.) He gulps down his food, because you know what's coming next. That's right—the evening news. And then there's another show, and... Before long, his little girl is coming up to his chair, hugging him, and saying "Good night, Daddy. I love you." *Is there much difference between this scene and the first?*

Building a Root System

What our children really need is a root system. If you did some digging in a redwood forest, you'd find that there are no taproots that go straight down. Instead, the roots go out from each tree and intertwine with the roots of surrounding trees. When a storm blows through that redwood forest, the well-developed root system enables the trees to support each other.

And that is exactly what families are supposed to do—form a root system together. Then, when the strong winds blow (and they *will* blow—especially during the years of adolescence), everybody in the family can brace and support each other. Now, how long do you think it took those redwood trees to develop that supporting root system? Do you think they did it in a few minutes of "quality time" per day? I think it took "quantity time."

The absence of this "quantity time" is one of the most notable features of American homes today. And it is the one thing this book will call for over and over. For without it, our missions are in jeopardy. A plane can fly on auto-pilot for a while, but when it's time to change course, to adjust for rough weather, to land... *the pilot has to be there!*

8   *The Circle of Influence*

Chapter 2

The Child Influencers

Particularly since World War II, many changes have occurred in patterns of child rearing in the United States, but their essence may be conveyed in a single sentence: *Children used to be brought up by their parents.*

It may seem presumptuous to put that statement in the past tense. Yet it does belong to the past. Over the years, *de facto* responsibility for upbringing has shifted away from the family to other settings in the society, some of which do not recognize or accept the task. While the family still has the primary moral and legal responsibility for the character development of children, it often lacks the power or opportunity to do the job, primarily because parents and children no longer spend enough time together in those situations in which such training is possible. This is not because parents do not want to spend time with their children. It is simply that conditions have changed.[1]

These words, written by the respected professor at Cornell University, Dr. Urie Bronfenbrenner, raise some important questions: What conditions have changed? Why does the family lack the power or opportunity to do the job? If parents are not bringing up their children, then who is? Or what is?

To understand the matter, we need to examine *the child influencers.* Imagine you are a child. With whom and what are you spending your time? Because you are young and impressionable, your thoughts, your actions, your view of the world, your very *self* will be affected by these influencers.

9

The Circle of Influence

In Figure 2.1, you see six major child influencers—television, peers, school, reading, parents, and family-based learning. There are others, but I believe these have been the most significant over the years. You see also that three of the influencers are in the *low parental control area*, while three are in the *high parental control area*. If, for instance, your child is watching TV, you don't know what the next scene or commercial will show him, and you therefore have little or no parental control. Likewise, your control is limited if he is in the park with his friends or listening to a lecture in health class at school.

If, however, your child is reading a book at home, you probably have read the book yourself or have a general idea of the contents. And if you are playing with your child or teaching him to tie his shoes, you certainly have a high level of parental control. I'm not suggesting that the level of

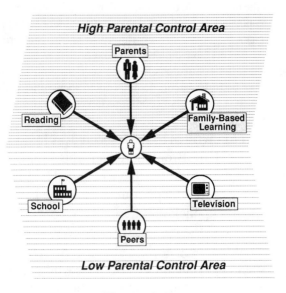

Figure 2.1

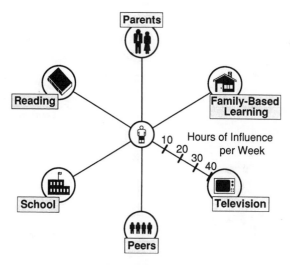

Figure 2.2

parental control should completely determine how your child spends his time. (You wouldn't want to totally eliminate the time your child spends with his friends.) But, in general, the less control you have as a parent, the less *you* will be rearing your child.

Now, let's look at the child influencers in terms of hours per week (Figure 2.2). During most of his waking hours, a child will be influenced by one of them. He will be watching TV, or talking with friends, or listening to his teacher, or reading a book... In some cases, he might be exposed to more than one influence at the same time—perhaps watching TV with his family. In such a case, we will ask what the major influencer is; that is, what has occupied most of his attention? With these ground rules, we are now ready to plot the number of hours per week—from 0 to 40—that the average child is exposed to each of the child influencers.

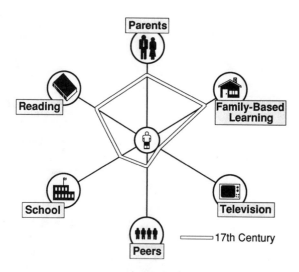

Figure 2.3

The 17th Century

The farther back in time we go, the fewer statistics, studies, and government reports we find. Therefore some estimation comes into play. I am, however, quite certain of one data point on Figure 2.3—no television was watched in the 17th century. Also, because we were primarily a rural society with primitive means of transportation, children spent a small portion of their time with children outside their homes. Professor Herbert Wright (University of Kansas) said:

> Unlike their urban and suburban age-mates, children in a small town become well acquainted with a substantially greater number of adults in different walks of life, and are more likely to be active participants in the adult settings which they enter.[2]

And 17th century education bore little semblance to the form it has taken today. Historian Arthur Calhoun said:

The colonial home was a little world... under whose roof the children could, if need were, learn all that was necessary for their future careers. The Puritans, as it has been seen, were strong for their training of children for their duties here and beyond.[3]

Even as late as 1870, the average number of school days attended per year was less than a third of what it is today (Figure 2.4[4]). Although these figures are not available for the 1600's and 1700's, you can imagine that the number of hours of influence per week from school was quite small.

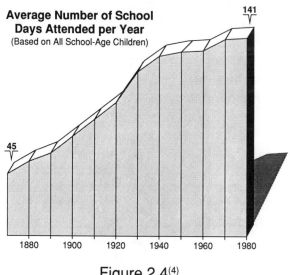

Average Number of School Days Attended per Year
(Based on All School-Age Children)

141

45

1880   1900   1920   1940   1960   1980

Figure 2.4[(4)]

What about the child influencers in the area of high parental control? The early-1700's diary of Cotton Mather included this:

I begin betimes to entertain them with delightful stories, especially Scriptural ones... And thus, every day at the table, I have used myself to tell a story before I rise; and made the story useful to the olive plants around the table.

When the children at any time accidently come in my way, it is my custom to let fall some sentence or other, that may be monitory and profitable to them...

I put them upon doing of services and kindnesses for one another, and for other children...

I first beget in them a high opinion of their father's love to them, and of his being best able to judge, what shall be good for them...

When the children are capable of it, I take them alone, one by one; and after my charges unto them, to fear God, and serve Christ...[5]

He read to them, he talked with them, he built character in them, he showed his love toward them, he guided them. In short, *he reared his own children.* Now, Cotton Mather may not have been the average father of that time. Yet, *by default,* since children were not being heavily influenced by TV, peers, and school, they had to be exposed more to the high-parental-control influencers.

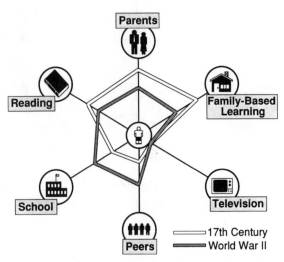

Figure 2.5

World War II Era

Think Waltons! Perhaps not a completely accurate way of looking at a bygone lifestyle, but for those of us young enough to have been raised on TV, it will have to do. You can see some serious shifts in influence had taken place by World War II (Figure 2.5). Television was still not affecting our children— it did not come into American homes until 1948. But children were now being influenced much more by their peers and school because the country was becoming more urbanized and now had mandatory education.

Every child has about 100 to 120 waking hours per week during which he will be influenced. Because more time was now being spent in the low parental control area, you can see that the influences of high parental control had to diminish. Yet even at this point, the average parent still played a large role in his child's development. Consider the following:

> My Daddy taught me young how to hunt and how to whittle,
> He taught me how to work and play a tune on the fiddle;
> He taught me how to love and how to give just a little,
> Thank God I'm a country boy.[6]

Why have I taken to reciting John Denver songs? The point is this: Today, if you wanted to learn how to whittle, you would probably have to take a continuing education course. And you'd likely learn how to play an instrument in band class.

Have you ever heard someone say, "That fellow's pretty handy"? In most cases, the ability to build and fix things is nothing more than an indication that a man's father took some time to teach him. This explains why so many men today don't feel "mechanically inclined." (In fact, if you quietly listen as they operate a screwdriver, you'll hear some men muttering, "Let's see... righty-tighty... lefty-loosey.")

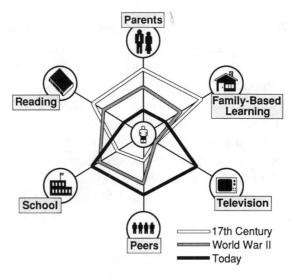

Figure 2.6

Today

Figure 2.6 sheds some light on Bronfenbrenner's conclusion, "Children used to be brought up by their parents." Television, an influence that did not even exist in the World War II era, is now, at over 31 hours per week, a major influence for the average American.[7] As we will later see, the influence exerted by peers and school is also extremely powerful.

So much for the influences of low parental control. What about reading, parents, and family-based learning? The U. S. Department of Education reported that grade-school children read silently for just 7 to 8 minutes per day at school; after school, half of all fifth-graders spend only 4 minutes a day reading.[8]

Particularly bleak is the picture we have of parents spending time with their children. In Figure 2.7[9] you see the paltry bit of time moms and dads spend conversing, reading, and playing with their children. What disturbs me is that *this is the*

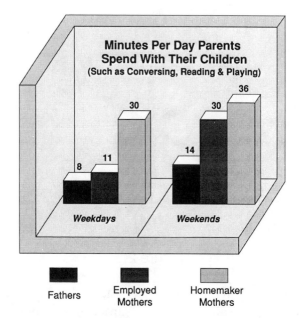

Figure 2.7[9]

most generous study I have seen. Other studies, particularly between fathers and their infant children, measure the time spent together in seconds per day!

What about family-based learning—chores, hobbies, learning a trade, repairwork, housework, character development, etc.? As we will see in Chapter 21, many parents have turned over the teaching of the useful things in life to the public school or Sunday School. No longer the center of learning, the home today is something like a combination of McDonald's, Holiday Inn, and Grand Central Station.

The Alarming Trend

In many ways, we have an "either-or" proposition on the lines shown in Figure 2.8. Either my daughters will pick up

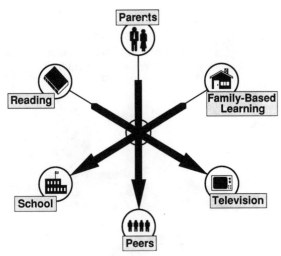

Figure 2.8

a book... or they'll turn on the TV. Either they'll spend some time on Saturday afternoon with Carol and me... or they'll go out to play with their friends. Either they'll learn how to bake a pie at home... or they'll learn this in home economics class. (To see how bizarre the situation is today, imagine one of our forefathers taking a tour through a school. He'd probably ask, "Why do you have these stoves and cooking supplies here to teach the girls? Don't you have these things in your homes?")

Are the downward trends shown in Figure 2.8 continuing, halting, or reversing? I believe they are continuing for most families. I can come to no other conclusion as I look at phenomena such as cable TV, VCR, pre-school, day-care centers, more employed moms, and busier parents.

But this need not be the case in your home. In Chapters 4 through 25, we'll look at each of these six influences in detail. And we won't just "curse the darkness," but will offer specific, positive suggestions you can implement in your home. So if you want to swim against the tide, if you want to have more of an influence on your child, *if you want to rear your own child*... then read on.

Chapter 3

Our Children Have Changed

"But kids are kids, and they really haven't changed much over the years." If I made this claim now, you'd be left scratching your head, wouldn't you? For if everything said in the last chapter was both *true* and *valid*, you would expect children to be much different today than even fifty years ago. Children simply cannot endure such massive changes in influence—from reading to TV, from home-based learning to institutional learning, from parents to peers—without being changed themselves.

So how have children changed? I agree with writer Neil Postman, that *childhood is disappearing.*[1] To a parent in my age group this might not be readily apparent because we know nothing other than that which now masquerades for childhood. To put the matter in perspective, let's examine some of the indicators that childhood is disappearing:

Few "Adult Secrets"—If you have watched TV commercials lately, you know that personal hygiene is no longer personal. And in so many other ways, children are losing the innocence of youth at earlier and earlier ages. The next time you speak to a 14-year-old, an 11-year-old, or even an 8-year-old, ask yourself, "Am I speaking to a child innocent of the secrets of adulthood, or am I speaking to a world-wise (and perhaps cynical) young adult?"

Kids in Entertainment—Do you remember the old Shirley Temple movies, in which she played a sweet, innocent little girl? That type of entertainment would never make prime time today. Instead, we have what has been called the "Gary Coleman syndrome," in which children no longer play little children, but rather miniature adults.

Kids in Advertising—Today, 12- and 13-year-old girls are among the highest-paid models in this country.[2] The pouty-faced, erotically-posed little girls in jeans commercials and ads are certainly not portraying little girls.

Language—Do you remember the language used around home when you were young? If someone spoke a foul word, Mom or Dad probably said, "Shhh—the children will hear!" Today it's a little different. Today, the children teach Mom and Dad the new words!

Games and Sports—In years gone by, children played hop scotch, hide-and-seek, red light-green light, jacks, spud, and freeze tag. Today, we dress them up in miniature adult football or baseball uniforms, send them out on the playing field, and scream at the ump if their team is losing. (I'm not saying we need to pull our kids out of Pee-Wee or Little League; we *do* need to make sure that childhood isn't pulled out of our kids.)

Children's Rights Movement—Children's rights advocate, Richard Farson, sees it this way:

> Children would... have the right to exercise determination in decisions about eating, sleeping, playing, listening, reading, washing, and dressing. They would have the right to choose their associates, the opportunity to decide what life goals they wish to pursue, and the freedom to engage in whatever activities are permissible for adults.[3]

He would give children the right to medical care without parental consent,[4] the right of full access to pornographic films and magazines,[5] and the right to alternative home environments if their parents don't suit them![6] Far out stuff? Yes, but not without echoes from high places. A federal judge advocates, "From the age of seven on, a youth should be able to exercise increasing control over his choice of school and work..."[7] She argues for an "emancipation proclamation... for teenage children."[8]

Clothing—Gone are the days when children wore clothes designed primarily for children, such as knickers. A casual glance through any clothing catalogue tells us that any adult style in dresses, jackets, or swim suits is now accepted in children's clothing. (And as the dividing line between childhood and adulthood blurs, it becomes common to see grandmas and grandpas in what used to be the uniform of youth—jeans and sneakers.)

Teen Pregnancy—I believe the number of unwanted teen pregnancies over the years is a solid indicator of whether or not children are changing. The appalling results are shown in Figure 3.1.[9] (To fairly treat these numbers, I must point out that there were unrecorded abortions prior to 1973. However, all indications are that the total number of unwanted teen

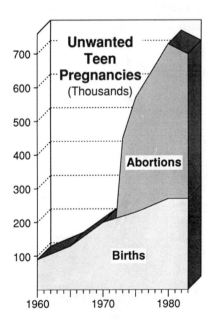

Figure 3.1[(9)]

pregnancies has soared over the decades.)

Crime—If at this point you have any doubt that children have substantially changed since the 1930's, Figure 3.2[10] should be helpful. In 1932, only 15,000 children were arrested *across this entire country*. Today the number stands above 1.5 million! Some might point out that there are more children today than in the 1930's. That's true. But there has been less than a three-fold increase in the number of children living, with more than a hundred-fold increase in the number of children arrested.

We could add many more items to this list—teen alcoholism...loss of respect for adults...street gangs...drug abuse...venereal disease...rebellion...suicide among children. But no matter how we view the situation, it is difficult to avoid this conclusion—childhood is disappearing. And I believe we can understand *why* it is disappearing by understanding the

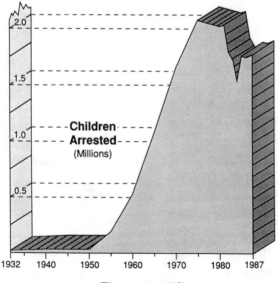

Figure 3.2[10]

change in the influences our children now face.

In the rest of this book, we will examine the six child influencers—television, reading, peers, parents, school, and family-based-learning—to gain this understanding. Much more importantly, we will look at changes we can make in our homes that will return childhood to our children and parenting to us.

Chapter 4

How Strong is the
Grip of Television?

It was a warm spring day in upper New York State. A perfect day for the four Davis children, aged 4, 7, 10, and 13 to be romping outside their family's large farmhouse. Were they climbing the many fruit trees nearby? Watching the fish swim in the clear stream behind their house? How about picking wild flowers, watching the squirrels, or looking down a wood-chuck hole? No, they were all sitting in a row on the sofa in their living room, staring at a small empty table. Why? A short time ago, before the TV antenna blew over, that table held the family TV.

"They really sat there for quite a while, just as if they were watching," their mother reported. "It was pathetic. But it made us absolutely certain that we'd done the right thing by chucking the set out."[1]

How strong is television's grip on the minds of children and their parents? When was the porch swing replaced by the TV? Where are we headed? These are questions we will examine in this chapter. In the next three chapters we will look at 1) the way television affects our brains, 2) some reasons to limit TV viewing, and 3) several suggestions to control it.

TV's Place in the Home Today

Statistics are not a major source of entertainment for most folks. But to get a clear picture of the position television now occupies in our lives, we need to go to the cold, hard numbers:

1) On average, 90 million Americans are watching TV on any given evening.[2]
2) By the time the average child graduates from kindergarten, he has watched 5000 hours of TV (enough for a bachelor's degree).[3]
3) The average high school graduate has watched between 15,000 and 22,000 hours of TV.[4]
4) 14-year-olds have witnessed 18,000 TV murders each, on average.[5]
5) The average American watches 4 hours and 28 minutes of TV per day.[6]

Let's think about that last statistic. That's over 31 hours per week... 1600 hours per year! Imagine what you could do with that much time. Learn a foreign language? Earn a college degree? Master a musical instrument?

For one final statistic on our viewing habits today, take a look at Figure 4.1.[7] Here we see that many children are still watching TV while you and I are probably counting sheep. From this, we know that many children watch television in an unrestricted and unsupervised manner. We haven't said whether TV viewing in itself is "bad" for us or our children. We'll leave that for the next two chapters. We do know at this point that, as a nation, we watch a *lot* of television.

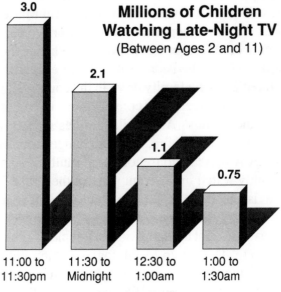

Figure 4.1[7]

The Ever-Tightening Grip of TV

One natural question is, "How long have we been watching so much TV?" You can see in Figure 4.2[8] that television sets didn't begin reaching American households until 1948. By 1949, a number of commentators were describing the benefits of this new technology for the family:

> Television is going to be a real asset in every home where there are children.[9]

> Television will take over your way of living and change your children's habits, but this change can be a wonderful improvement.[10]

> No survey's needed, of course, to establish that television has brought the family together in one room.[11]

Although nearly three decades passed before many of the negative effects of TV were first revealed (in Marie Winn's book, *The Plug-In Drug*), these writers were correct in this: Television would forever and irreversibly change the American family. The television replaced more than the porch swing. It replaced the family drive in the country, it replaced family games, and it replaced conversations in the parlor with neighbors and friends. And while families *started* watching TV in the same living room, that has changed too. By 1980, over half of American households had multiple sets so they could silently watch in different parts of the house.[12]

What is the outlook for the future? Not many more families can buy their first TV. That's because 98% already own at least one. But the same cannot be said of cable TV and VCR's... yet. These two technologies, which increase our overall viewing time, are now invading American homes in the same way TV did in the 1950's (Figure 4.2).

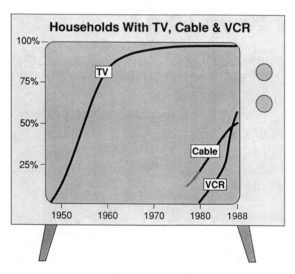

Figure 4.2[8]

Finally, to understand the true impact of television, we have to look beyond just the number of families with sets. We have to see how families have been using those sets. As shown in Figure 4.3, the average television was turned on 2.5 hours per day *more* in 1988 than it was in 1950.[13] (While the average set is on 7.1 hours per day, the average person watches approximately 4.5 hours per day.)

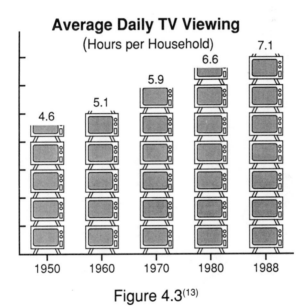

Average Daily TV Viewing
(Hours per Household)

Figure 4.3[13]

To summarize, we watch a lot of TV and we are watching more all the time. We have already reached the point where the average child spends more time watching TV than doing *anything* else except sleeping![14]

You may say, "That's all interesting, but I don't watch *that* much." You're probably right. The very fact that you are now reading a book suggests you are below the national average in TV viewing time. But the real question doesn't deal with national averages. It deals with you. You may be wondering how much time, if any, is the "right" amount of time for you and yours to watch TV. I can't give an answer for any family other than mine. I do believe we must become informed of the effects of TV, and then prayerfully chart our course of action. The next two chapters are aimed at helping you become informed.

Chapter 5
TV and Your Brain Waves

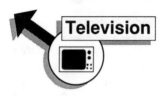

Several years ago, the following letter was received by Abigail Van Buren:

Dear Abby:
This may sound crazy, but I need your advice. I am divorced and the mother of a sweet, 4-year-old boy named Ronnie.

We were at home recently when an armed intruder confronted us. The man was gentle, and he quickly put Ronnie at ease. He wanted only money and promised not to hurt us. We both explained to Ronnie that Mommy would have to be tied up for a while. He seemed to understand.

After I was bound and gagged, Ronnie was told to turn the TV on and when the program was over (about 20 minutes) he could help me or call for help. I was taken to another room and the robber left.

Abby, my son spent the next three hours watching TV, while I was bound and utterly helpless. I finally managed, through the gag, to tell him to go next door for help.

Could Ronnie possibly have some hostility toward me? Should I see a psychologist? Please answer.[1]

- "Tied Up"

Dimming Out the World

Do you have a "little Ronnie" in your home? Do your children seem to be in a trance when they are watching TV? There is good reason for this. When someone watches television, he can enter an *altered state of consciousness*. Here is the way this process is described by Dr. Karl Albrecht, author of *Brain Power*:

> A number of investigations have shown that, after spending about 30 minutes or more staring into a television screen at typical programming material, a viewer's brain is in a condition qualitatively similar to hypnosis. The body becomes more or less inert, with markedly diminished kinetic processes. Respiration and heart rate may decline somewhat. Attention narrows to include only the images on the screen and the sounds coming from the speaker. Shifting attention to other events or processes in the room requires an unwanted mental effort. The popularity of automatic channel-selecting devices, operable from the easy chair, probably stems from this condition of quasi-hypnosis more than from any supposed characteristic of "laziness" on the part of the viewer. From the point of view of brain activity, passivity is self-reinforcing. The longer one remains fixated on a sensory process that requires little or no active thought, the more fixated one is likely to become, until it takes a moderate effort to break out of the semitrance condition.[2]

To see how this works, try watching a 30-minute program while you are standing up. Don't lean against the wall or couch. You will probably find you are more aware of what is going on around you than you normally are when watching TV. If there are others who are watching TV with you, compare their state of "fixation" to yours. You may also find that you are more observant and critical of what you are watching, especially the commercials.

One of the effects of TV, then, is that we "dim out" our surroundings. Imagine this scene: You are in your living room watching TV from a comfortable chair. The room is dark. Everyone has been "trained" to keep interruptions to a minimum. Because the TV is at the other side of the room and measures only inches across, your gaze is fixed within a narrow range. The sound coming from the TV is also in a narrow range. Your use of other senses—smell, taste and touch—is eliminated. Finally, you have put yourself in a comfortable position that will require the least possible movement. Even your heart and lungs have slowed their pace somewhat.

Are you getting the picture? You have effectively dimmed out the world around you. In fact you have even partially dimmed out your own body as you fixed your gaze on a single object. *Without knowing it, you have gone through the same basic steps that a hypnotist would perform.*

300,000 Dots at 30 Images Per Second

Imagine you are still in your easy chair and watching *The Bill Cosby Show*. As you sit there, you think you are watching an image of Bill Cosby. But you are not. Instead you are looking at the phosphorescent glow of three hundred thousand dots which are being rapidly turned on and off.

As shown in Figure 5.1, the dots are lit sequentially beginning in the upper right-hand corner of your screen. Depending on the image projected, the dots are turned on or off as the scanning system moves down the screen, one row at a time. By the time the scan reaches Bill's chin, the dots making up his forehead are already fading. That is why there is never an image of Bill Cosby on the screen. It only looks like an image of Bill Cosby because these scans take place so quickly—30 per second. *Unlike life around us, where what you see actually exists, TV images only take place after you have assembled them in your brain.*

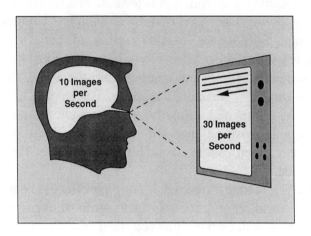

Figure 5.1

God equipped us with brains that can only detect 10 images per second. That is all that is needed in nature. (I suppose He felt that if we saw a charging rhino 10 times each second...that would be *plenty*.) If something is happening faster than that, the nerves between our retinas and brains cannot process it, so it blends into a continuous motion. That is why TV, with its 30 images per second, appears to portray continuous motion instead of strobe-like images.

While this technology works well with the conscious mind, we now know that it can have a *subliminal* effect on the sub-conscious mind. A subliminal message is one that enters and affects the brain without alerting the conscious mind. In effect, the mind tries to keep up with the rapid TV imagery, but finally "gives up." According to author Jerry Mander, "Eventually, the conscious mind gives up noting the process and merges with the experience. The body vibrates with the beat and the mind gives itself over, opening up to whatever imagery is offered."[3] (Pretty soon it's *harrrooooooooooooom*— without the lotus position and outstretched hands.)

Inside the Brain

So, what is actually happening inside our brains when they are in their "TV mode"? Let's begin by looking at the differences between the right and left hemispheres. The left hemisphere is the center of our logic, reading, analysis and speaking; it operates on a *sequential* basis. (If A = B and B = C, then A = C.) The right hemisphere is the center of our dream images, spatial awareness, fantasy and intuition. It operates on a *non-sequential* basis.

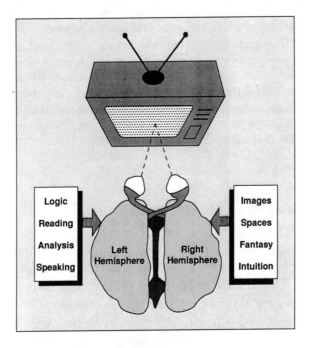

Because the right hemisphere is visually oriented, it has no problem taking in the images of television. The problem comes when the information in those images is transferred to the left hemisphere. This process has been studied by a team of researchers headed by psychologists Merrelyn and Fred Emery at the Australian National University at Canberra.

Their work centered on the left cortex and particularly area thirty-nine, the "common integrative area," which is the center of logic, analysis, and memory.

According to the Emerys, evidence shows that humans *habituate* to repetitive light-stimuli; this happens with flickering light, dot patterns, and limited eye movement. Mander summarizes their findings on this brain process:

> If habituation occurs, then the brain has essentially decided that there is nothing of interest going on—at least nothing that anything can be done about—and virtually quits processing the information that goes in. In particular... the left-brain "common integrative area" goes into a kind of holding pattern...
>
> The right half of the brain, which deals with more subjective cognitive processes—dream images, fantasy, intuition—continues to receive the television images. But because the bridge between the right and left brains has been effectively shattered, all cross-processing, the making conscious of the unconscious data and bringing it into usability, is eliminated. *The information goes in, but it cannot be easily recalled or thought about.*[4] (Italics mine)

Measuring Brain Wave Activity

How do we know TV viewing affects the brain in this manner? At least two researchers have independently confirmed TV-induced changes in brain wave activity using electroencephalographic (brain wave) testing.

In both cases they noted changes in the types of brain waves—*alpha* vs. *beta*. Alpha waves occur when the mind is not orienting to something. These brain waves are slow and typical of the person who is "spaced out," passive, and unaware of the outside world. These same alpha waves, recorded over the back part of the scalp, disappear as soon as the person begins orienting to somebody or something. Then, the faster beta waves become predominant.

Have you ever noticed, while reading, that you hadn't really absorbed anything in the last paragraph or two? (Maybe this is happening right now.) You probably had to go back over the sentences that your *eyes* had read but that your *mind* had not. When this happened, your mind slipped from its normal beta wave activity to a non-orienting alpha wave mode. Then it said, "Whoops, I must have slipped into alpha," and you re-read the passage using beta waves.

These wave forms were studied in TV-viewers by Dr. Erik Peper, a widely published researcher on electroencephalographic testing at MIT and San Francisco State University. He describes his experiment as follows:

> Ten kids were asked to watch their favorite television programs. Our assumption was that since these programs were their favorite shows, the kids would be involved in them and we'd find there'd be an oscillation between alpha slow-wave activity and beta. The prediction was that they would go back and forth. But they didn't do that. They just sat back. They stayed almost all the time in alpha. This meant that while they were watching they were not reacting, not orienting, not focusing, just spaced-out.[5]

By comparison, Dr. Peper noted that reading produces a much higher level of beta activity. He added,

> The horror of television is that the information goes in, but we don't react to it. It goes right into our memory pool and perhaps we react to it later but we don't know what we're reacting to. When you watch television you are training yourself not to react and so later on, you're doing things without knowing why you're doing them or where they came from.[6]

The real message of this chapter, then, is this: *We give up a measure of control over our thinking process due to the nature of the media itself.* Normally we focus, if at all, on the content of the programs we and our children watch. And while that is so very important, the problem runs deeper. For everything we watch, commercials included, can pour through the unguarded gate of the mind, and rest there in the subconscious mind for later use.

And once an image is lodged in your mind, how do you dislodge it? Close your eyes and picture Captain Kirk, Archie Bunker, Hawkeye, or Radar. Have you ever met these people? Are they even *real*? Yet there they reside, forever, in your mind, along with your mother and father... your spouse... your children.

Chapter 6

19 Reasons to Limit TV Viewing

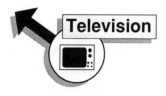

Five years ago, we had a spring porch sale that began in typical fashion. Carol sat at the card table answering questions and collecting money. Jennifer, then 5, and Katie, 3, rediscovered old toys. I milled around, surprised that anybody would actually pay for our junk, and just as perplexed that nobody was buying our treasures. Every now and then, we'd greet a visiting forager with, "See anything you can't live without?"

This day also included our usual expeditions into the house to find one more artifact we *could* live without. And this day we hit the jackpot. We returned to the porch lugging two TV sets.

When I talk about pitching the TVs, I don't speak as an expert who's got it all together. I speak as a coward who got it out. Since our marriage, Carol had been watching TV less and less, as were our girls. (Carol cut out the daytime viewing when Jennifer knew all the characters on one soap opera— which she called *The Young and the Rest-of-Us*.) On the other hand, I had been watching more. So when the opportunity came, we called the girls in from the porch and talked to them about life without TV. We told them it would be one in which

Mommy and Daddy would spend more time with them.

And with the TVs gone, it *was* easier to spend that time together. On many evenings, the family would choose between playing a board game, having a sing-a-long, or reading together. It wasn't long before Carol and I began to feel that we knew our girls a lot better. (In fact, after a month, I was able to take off their nametags!)

Now, if you feel a "dump the TV" sermon coming on, don't panic. The title for this chapter speaks of *limiting*—not necessarily *eliminating*—the TV. In the next chapter, we will look at several ways to do this limiting. But first, the reasons...

Reason #1: TV Can Be Addicting

Television doesn't affect everyone in the same way. For this reason I don't feel comfortable giving a "one-size-fits-all" solution for TV control. One person may only flip the set on once or twice a month, while another may watch so much TV that his eyes begin to get rectangular-shaped.

I see several similarities for some people between TV viewing and chemical addiction. First, the real world is blotted out. To see this, watch your glassy-eyed family the next time they are engrossed in a TV program. Or better yet, try to carry on a conversation and watch what a strain it is for them to pull their eyes away.

Secondly, like an addict, the TV viewer often overestimates his control of his addiction. Many times I remember turning the TV on, thinking that I would just watch for "a little while." Hours later, I would drag myself off to bed. Now and then I meet somebody suffering from sleep deprivation and they say, "But I can turn that thing off whenever I want to. Sure. No problem. I *wanted* to watch till 1:30 this morning."

Finally, other activities revolve around the addiction—in this case the TV. We have entire industries which stand as testimony to this fact: TV trays... portable TVs... TV dinners. Many folks adjust their eating schedule, their visiting, their family time, and any other "obstacles" around the TV schedule. *Sadly, some miss their lives so they don't miss their shows.*

Reason #2: TV Can Interfere With Learning

Several years ago the California Department of Education gave a scholastic achievement test to sixth- and twelfth-grade students. Buried in the test, the students found the question, "How much time do you spend watching TV each day?" Author Jim Trelease describes the results:

> When the educators finished compiling the scores on the 500,000 exams, they began to correlate each child's grade with the number of hours the student spent watching television. Their findings showed conclusively that the more time the student spent watching TV, the lower the achievement score; the less time, the higher the score. Interestingly, these statistics proved true regardless of the child's IQ, social background, or study practices (all of which were queried in the exam process)[1]

In another study, researchers measured the reading skills of 9-, 13- and 17-year-olds.[2] Data was collected on the amount of TV watched and the availability of reading materials in the home. You can see the results in Figure 6.1. A 9-year-old who watches little TV, but has many reading materials available, would have nearly the same reading proficiency as a 13-year-old with a lot of TV and few reading materials. For the 13-year-old, that's a four year loss!

Keep in mind that these studies only deal with averages. They can't predict the outcome of TV viewing on your child's academic success. But they strongly suggest that your child will be helped academically by limiting TV viewing.

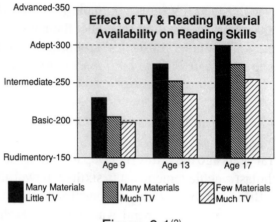

Figure 6.1[2]

Reason #3: TV Can Discourage Reading

Because they are both forms of quiet, indoor entertainment, TV viewing and reading often compete with each other for the hours of our children's lives. TV is winning. It may be because TV viewing is easier, or perhaps it's due to the role models offered by parents. Whatever the reasons, TV's relative popularity is clear. In one study, when second-graders were offered the same story on TV and in book form, 69% chose television. Among third-graders, the figure jumped to 86%. It's probably no coincidence that by third grade our reading skills as a nation begin to plummet.[3]

It may not seem that our children's preference for TV over books is such a big deal. In Chapter 8, we will examine some significant differences between the two media.

Reason #4: TV Viewing Can Hinder Writing Skills

One of our country's great writers, E. B. White, didn't sugar-coat his feelings about TV when he said, "Short of throwing away all the television sets, I really don't know what we can do about writing."[4]

Study after study has shown an alarming decline in the ability of our youth to assemble their thoughts on paper in a coherent, logical fashion. Is Mr. White correct in laying the blame on the family TV? Quite possibly. Because the TV plays more to the spatially-oriented right brain, it is likely that the verbally-oriented left brain becomes under-developed during thousands of hours of childhood TV viewing. If so, you would expect college verbal test scores to have begun dropping 10 to 15 years after those students—as young children—had started watching TV on a massive scale. This is exactly what has happened (Figure 6.2[5]).

This is not proof of a cause and effect relationship, and I personally believe there have also been other causes for this

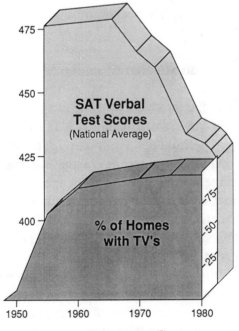

Figure 6.2[5]

academic slide. But surely some control is warranted lest we allow tomorrow's writers to spend much of their childhood at the feet of the flickering instructor.

Reason #5: TV Can Promote Easy Answer Problem Solving

You know how this works. Most major crimes and domestic problems can be solved in 30 or 60 minutes. It takes 15 or 30 seconds to dispatch difficulties such as stubborn grass stains, split ends, or a nagging cough.

Sure, we all know that these problems take more time to resolve than the standard TV program or commercial affords. And if we were just occasionally exposed to this condensed problem solving, it probably wouldn't affect us. But what about the average 18-year-old who has spent more of his waking hours watching TV than doing anything else?

Reason #6: TV Can Shorten Attention Spans

If you were the producer of a television program or commercial, you would try to include as many *technical shifts* as your budget permitted. Examples of technical shifts include the zoom, fade-out, scene change, superscript, slow motion, new camera angle, and sound change. The reason you would use these is that the television medium is inherently boring. Video detail and depth of field and even audio quality are actually poor substitutes for the real world. (When was the last time you admired a televised sunset?)

Technical shifts are therefore added to grab your attention. Because this is done so frequently, it has the effect of breaking your attention into a succession of short segments. Most advertising includes 20 to 30 technical shifts per minute while commercial programming contains 8 to 10.[6] Public television has historically incorporated only 2 to 3 shifts per minute.[7] (Imagine sitting in your living room watching the wildebeests on the plains of the Serengeti for 30 seconds a pop. That's why many folks don't watch much public TV.)

Sesame Street, unlike most public TV programming, is packed full of technical shifts.[8] At the risk of going from preaching to meddling, I'd like to discuss *Sesame Street* a little further. The program first aired in 1969 and quickly became watched by about one-half of all 3-5 year olds.[9] In fairness to the program, it may improve the reading readiness of children who watch it. (1970 and 1971 studies by the Educational Testing Service showed that young viewers made gains. In 1975, however, a team of social scientists found that the gains due to *Sesame Street* were marginal and suspect.)[10]

Typically, however, children lose any such gains in reading readiness by the 1st or 2nd grade.[11] Unfortunately, what the child may retain are poor learning habits. According to the producer, "We stole everything from *Laugh-In*."[12] By using techniques such as instant replay, unrelated rapid-fire segments, and stop action, the show can promote short attention spans. The child may develop a passive "entertain me" approach to learning after a steady diet of "Pow! Zap! Whammo!" Then he goes to his kindergarten class and in walks a silver-haired, grandmotherly teacher. Guess what? No "Pow! Zap! Whammo!"

Reason #7: TV Doesn't Promote Active Thinking

Over 20 years ago, the CBS vice-president of children's programming told an interviewer that he had not allowed his own children to watch TV during the week while growing up. The TV executive said that he had compelled his children "to do something more intellectually alive."[13]

Has the quality of programming improved since then? Probably not. TV is an enormously hungry medium, with TV stations operating up to 24 hours per day, 7 days per week, and 52 weeks per year. They require a huge supply of broadcast material which has not exactly led to a high standard of mind-stimulating substance. The "history" of broadcasting is summarized by Dr. Karl Albrecht:

> Television had gained a central place in American life by about 1960. By 1970, TV scriptwriters had run out of material. Of course, that didn't slow them down. They merely continued to redo the same basic material—human interest situations with simplified plots—in different forms. They substituted one cadre of stock characters for the previous set, changed the story lines a bit, readjusted the ratio of sex to violence, and brought out the next season's series.[14]

Television has been called "chewing gum for the mind." (Watching TV relates to active thinking in about the same way that chewing a wad of gum relates to talking: part of the same apparatus is involved but there is no output.) The viewer is in a "trancelike stupor in which active thinking becomes an unwanted distraction from a narrowly fixated sensory state."[15] (Albrecht)

It is largely because of this condition that TV program schedules look the way they do. Pick up your *TV Guide* and try a simple test. Count the number of documentaries and educational programs. Now compare that to the number of situation comedies, dramas, movies, soap operas, and sport events. Mind-stimulating or mind-numbing?

We must even question what many consider to be the great redeeming factor in TV—the nightly news. I timed the news coverage one evening and here is what I found:[16]

Time (seconds)	News Story
173	Waste treatment plant to close
49	Jet makes emergency landing
25	Plane crashes in Georgia
31	President discusses hostages
53	School officials found guilty
30	Jury deliberating rape charges
23	Police search for murderer
27	Man indicted in burning attack
68	Ten-year-old accused of murder
48	Testimony of witness questioned
106	Airline flies despite strike
25	FBI investigation wraps up
24	U.S. Defense budget passed
16	New missile tested
33	Three blimps fly together

The program devoted a whopping average of 49 seconds to each story. How much active, deep thinking can we do in 49 seconds? We have enough time to absorb the event, but not enough time to really think it through. *Perception* can take place, but not *conception.*

Contrast this with the type of thinking that would have taken place years ago in parlors across this nation. Friends, neighbors, and family would discuss their political views, their philosophy, and their faith, unfettered by the second hand in a television studio.

Reason #8: TV Hinders Creative Play and Exploration

Researchers questioned how best to stimulate children's creativity: With an adult or with a TV? Even with the show, *Mr. Rogers*, the greatest gains in imaginative play occurred with an involved adult and no television:[17]

Group	Watching TV	Adult Presence	Imaginative Play
1	Yes	None	Little or no gain
2	Yes	Adult mediator	Some gain
3	No	Teacher & games	Greatest increase
4	No	None	Little or no gain

Ideally, we would like to compare the creativity of children who never watch TV to the creativity of those that do. But there is a problem: We can't find the children who don't watch any TV!

However, we can look at what Marie Winn called an "experiment of nature." In the 1970's, she interviewed nursery and kindergarten teachers who were old enough to have taught both pre- and post-TV kids. Here was a typical observation from one of those teachers:

> There's been a move from active, impulsive kids who were just very eager to get their hands on things to do, to more cautious, passive kids with attitudes of wanting to be entertained or instructed. They don't want to just go ahead and explore by themselves.[18]

And the reason they don't just go ahead and explore by themselves is that they are so used to sitting in front of their TVs. Mothers of first-graders were asked what their children would do with the extra time if TV didn't exist. Ninety percent said they would be playing.[19]

Reason #9: TV Promotes a Distorted View of the Real World

For many viewers, fictional TV personalities take on lives of their own. Do you remember the *Marcus Welby, M.D.* show, in which Robert Young played the gentle doctor? During the first five years of his "practice," he received

250,000 letters, most of which asked for medical advice.[20] These viewers had mistaken a member of the Screen Actors' Guild for a member of the American Medical Association!

Drs. Gross and Gerbner tried to better understand how TV programming twists our view of the world.[21] To do this, they asked several questions of both heavy TV viewers and light TV viewers. When asked the likelihood of encountering violence in any one week, most light viewers correctly estimated the chances to be 100:1 against it. The heavy viewers, however, generally said the odds were 10:1 against, or even 50:50. After all, it's a rough world out there, right? Why, every week there are dozens of mob figures (or street thugs or bad spies) for the detectives (or policemen or good spies) to high-speed-chase (or apprehend or blow-away.) Of course, these are interchangeable for "variety."

What's more, the heavy TV viewers pegged the U.S. proportion of the world population much too high. They also thought there was a higher-than-actual percentage of the real world employed as athletes, entertainers, and professionals.

As TV is watched more and more, it can take on proportions that seem larger than life itself. I chuckled as I read the account of a 17-year old boy who had just survived a tornado: "Man, it was just like something on TV."[22]

Reason #10: TV Commercials Exploit Children

Society has long recognized the need to shelter the naive child from the experienced hustler. But, in the case of television commercials, the floodgates have been opened as wide as possible. A concerned doctor, Michael Rothenberg, once brought the matter into focus:

> Twenty-five percent of the television industry's profits comes from the 7 percent of its programming directed at children.

> While the Code of Hammurabi in 2250 BC made selling some-
> thing to a child or buying something from a child without power
> of attorney a crime punishable by death, in 1975 AD our children
> are exposed to some 350,000 television commercials by the time
> they reach age 18, promising super-power, sugar-power, toy-
> power, and kid-power.[23]

It's shocking to realize that our children watch an average of *5 hours of advertising per week.*[24] In addition, they are exposed to many cartoons which are little more than half-hour commercials. I believe what we need here is a little suspended animation. (That's when the kids aren't allowed to watch cartoons.)

Perhaps most sobering is the relationship between our children's viewing patterns and their behavior. A RAND Corporation compendium, for instance, listed more than 20 studies that showed a positive correlation between heavy TV commercial viewing and children's use of over-the-counter drugs.[25] Over-the-counter drugs are among the most heavily advertised products on TV today.

Reason #11: TV Can Cause Anxiety Symptoms

This is a problem that probably does not affect a large portion of young TV viewers, yet reveals the dark potential of TV. At two U.S. Air Force base hospitals, doctors examined 30 children who were suffering from chronic fatigue, loss of appetite, headaches, and vomiting.[26] All the children watched a lot of TV: 3-6 hours per weekday and 6-10 hours per day on the weekends.

The doctors instructed the families to stop watching TV. For those 12 children that did, the symptoms were gone in 2-3 weeks. For the other 18 children, TV viewing was reduced to less than 2 hours per day and the symptoms disappeared in 3-6 weeks.

The link between TV and the symptoms became even stronger after follow-up visits. The 9 children for whom TV was still restricted were free of their symptoms. Four children who watched TV on a limited basis began having limited symptoms. Out of 13 children who had returned to their earlier viewing habits, 11 once again had severe symptoms. Sadly, those parents were not able to control TV viewing even when it jeopardized their children's health.

Reason #12: TV Can Promote Poor Physical Fitness

While anxiety symptoms may be a rare effect of TV viewing, obesity is not. In fact, you can almost predict how your child will "grow with the experience."

> In a study of approximately 7000 6-to-11-year-olds and nearly as many adolescents, 12 to 17, Drs. Dietz and Gortmaker found that for both age groups, but particularly adolescents, youngsters who watch the most TV on a daily basis are significantly more obese or super-obese than their peers who watch less TV.
>
> In fact, say the two researchers, the prevalence of obesity increases by 2 percent for each additional hour adolescents view television.[27]

This should not surprise us. Look at all the tempting food shown during commercials. (I used to feel like one of Pavlov's dogs during that commercial showing a sundae dish floating on a chocolate sea past ice cream mountains.) And when children watch TV, they aren't running and climbing and jumping. They are sitting and stuffing and munching.

Reason #13: TV Can Cause Family Conflict

In 1980, the Roper organization asked 4000 husbands and wives their most frequent subject of fights.[28] Television and children tied for second place. At first this stumped me; then I realized it was probably the "I-wanna-watch-my-show" syndrome. As a nation, we are rapidly moving to solve this problem, however. We are buying more sets and retiring to our individual bedroom and family-room cocoons to watch them in peace.

Reason #14: TV Violence Promotes Aggressive Behavior

Thirteen-year-old Juan Valdez confessed to being one of two teen-agers who ambushed the father of a friend in his own home, and then kicked, stabbed, and beat him with a fireplace poker, before choking him to death. Why, police wanted to know, after all that, did they pour salt into the victim's wounds?

"Oh, I don't know," the teen replied, "I just seen it on TV."[29]

Wait a minute, you may say. You can't blame TV for our nation's violence based on a few isolated cases. True. But of the 85 major studies on the subject, only one concluded that TV violence did *not* cause increased aggression in children. That study was paid for by NBC. (Later, independent researchers concluded that the network-hired researchers had misinterpreted their own evidence, and that the data *did* show a causal relationship between TV violence and children's aggression.)[30]

In fact, the relationship of television violence to aggressive behavior is so clear that:

1) some child psychologists can tell after one visit if a child watches violent TV,[31]

2) researchers concluded that violent TV viewing was the strongest predictor of violent behavior—ahead of factors such as parents' behavior, poverty, and race,[32] and

3) one expert attributes up to one half of the murders committed in the U.S. and Canada to the effects of TV.[33]

Murder statistics probably aren't your chief concern as you think about your child in front of the TV. A little closer to home are the phenomena called *novel aggressive behavior sequences.* I had a hard time picturing novel aggressive behavior sequences for a while. Then I got caught in the toy store cross-fire of two boys pretending to be something akin to a well-armed GI Joe with Ninja ancestry.

The fact is, if you want to see the most TV violence, you need to be a child—or at least watch their shows. Let's say you had the strange goal of seeing 54 acts of violence. You could a) watch all 37 Shakespeare plays, b) watch 2-3 evenings of prime-time TV, or (if you want to be efficient with your time) c) watch one hour of Saturday morning cartoons.[34]

Reason #15: TV Negatively Portrays Christians

For years the networks have depicted Christians in an unflattering manner. According to writer Kevin Perrota:

> Most Christians portrayed on television fall into one of three types: The gentle, slightly muddled, and highly ineffectual preacher (Father Mulcahey, the Catholic chaplain in "M*A*S*H*", was once stunned when one of his prayers actually "worked" and a sick patient recovered.)

The fast-talking, Bible-thumping, and probably money-grubbing, Elmer Gantry type of evangelist.
The spaced-out cult member.[35]

It's true that believers struggle in this world and some stumble badly. But the TV programmers have distorted the shortcomings of God's people well beyond reasonable proportions. This can really damage the self-concept of a young Christian who is looking at the world around him through the filtered eyes of television.

Reason #16: TV Condones Immorality

It seems the objective of many TV producers is to break as many of the 10 commandments as possible in the allotted 30 or 60 minutes. You know the scene. A couple is sitting poolside. She bears false witness against a friend, he covets his neighbor's wife, and so on.

As cable TV and the networks wrestle in the mud for ratings, our living rooms are increasingly becoming front row seats to nudity, foul language, and graphic violence. And most of us watch and say, "There were a few bad scenes, but overall it wasn't too bad." After the 100th time we heard that a movie or TV show wasn't too bad, Carol said to me, "Not *too bad*! Why doesn't anybody ask if it's *good enough*?"

Can you imagine what the following would do to the Nielsen ratings?

Finally, brothers, whatever is true, whatever is noble, whatever is right, whatever is pure, whatever is lovely, whatever is admirable—if anything is excellent or praiseworthy—think about such things.[36]

Don't hold your breath waiting for graduates from the Philippians 4:8 School of Directing. Network executives know the noble, the pure, and the lovely aren't going to compete well with the disgusting, the erotic, and the profane for the attention of jaded America. I'm not saying we shouldn't try to change the output of network directors. I'm saying we must change the input of our children's minds. We've got to be the gatekeepers. It's our job and nobody else can do it. Few even want to.

To put this whole subject in perspective, let's go back to the early days of *The Tonight Show*. Then host, Jack Paar used the expression "W.C." one evening, which stood for water closet (the toilet). It created such a stir among the network brass that Paar later quit in tears.

It disturbs me to see how far and how fast we've slipped. But it *scares* me when I think how easily, how comfortably we've slipped. It makes the words of C. S. Lewis from *The Screwtape Letters* seem to shout:

> Indeed the safest road to hell is the gradual one—the gentle slope, soft underfoot, without sudden turnings, without milestones, without signposts.[37]

Reason #17: TV Erodes the Dividing Line Between Childhood and Adulthood

TV is one of the major causes for the disappearance of childhood. It actually erodes the dividing line between childhood and adulthood, and it does this in two ways.

First, television does not segregate its audience. Before the electronic media age, children remained children partly because they didn't have much access to adult information. Years of study were required to master the skill of reading. Today, virtually unlimited access to adult information can be had by any child who has mastered the skill of button-pressing. The result is that a child of three can be exposed to such talk show patter as, "Don't go away. We'll be back with a marvelous new diet and, then, a quick look at incest."[38]

Secondly, TV makes no complex demands on the mind. (This is probably the understatement of the chapter.) It has been said that no advertiser ever lost money underestimating the intelligence of the American public. I've found this maxim particularly dear to the hearts of pick-up truck advertisers. Once, during a football play-off game, I called everyone's attention to the commercial then playing.

"Look," I said, "An adult-level pickup truck commercial. You will note that they have not dropped this truck from a helicopter into a net, driven it down roller coaster tracks, or burst it into a ball of flames."

The salesman was calmly extolling the truck's virtues as he sat in the truck bed. Then, as my friends watched the commercial ending, the camera angle panned back to show his truck sitting on another truck which was sitting on another truck...

The bottom line is children and adults now watch programming aimed at *both* groups. And they enjoy it, with children's favorite shows repeatedly showing up on lists of adults' favorite shows.[39] This is leading us into a blended society of "childified" adults and "adultified" children.

Reason #18: TV Undermines Parental Influence

We'd like to think that what our children see on TV is soon forgotten and won't come back to haunt us or them later. After a review of the research, however, Mankiewicz and Swerdlow concluded, "Children are more likely to model themselves upon what they have seen on film than they are to follow verbal instructions from a real, physically present parent."[40]

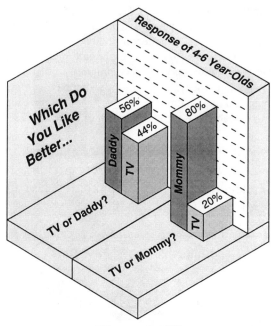

Figure 6.3[(41)]

Not only do children model TV programs, some like those programs better than Mom or Dad. Children, age 4 to 6, were asked who they liked best, 1) TV or Daddy, and 2) TV or Mommy? The depressing results are shown in Figure 6.3.[41] Why? Most children spend far more time with their TVs than their parents.

Reason #19: TV Displaces Living!

For many, this is one of the strongest reasons for "doing something" about the TV. Many have said it, but none have said it better than education expert, Dr. Paul Copperman:

Consider what a child misses during the 15,000 hours he spends in front of the TV screen. He is not working in the garage with his father, or in the garden with his mother. He is not doing homework, or reading, or collecting stamps. He is not cleaning his room, washing the supper dishes, or cutting the lawn. He is not listening to a discussion about community politics among his parents and their friends. He is not playing baseball, or going fishing, or painting pictures. Exactly what does television offer that is so valuable that it can replace all of these activities?[42]

For a picture of this, take a look at Figure 6.4.[43] You can see that TV viewing time dwarfs other activities. It is like a huge time bandit, robbing our children of their time, their learning, and even their childhood.

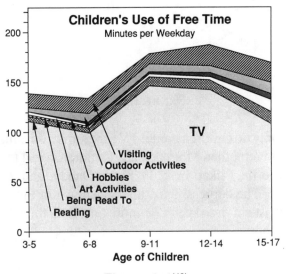

Figure 6.4[(43)]

Perhaps wading through 19 reasons to limit the TV is overkill. Certainly not all of the reasons will apply to your family, but if you recognize some traps that have caught you and yours, don't be discouraged. Other families have been caught and have unsprung their traps by taking some simple steps. So take heart and read on.

Chapter 7
TV: What to Do... What to Do...

I knew a father who had finally become fed up with his TV. I don't remember if it was the violence, the hours wasted, or the immorality. (I know it wasn't the reception.) At any rate, he took his TV to the backyard and placed it on a stump. After gathering together family and friends, he produced a 12-gauge shotgun and dispatched his set in a most convincing manner. In the military vernacular, I suppose you could say he "fired for effect."

While I wouldn't drape my body over your TV set to protect it, I think there are some other—though less dramatic— ways you might want to deal with TV viewing. Our family has tried a number of approaches to limit our TV viewing, and we found some worked better than others. I've included these, with a few tactics others have tried, for you to consider.

Approach #1: "I'll Try to Do Better"

This is probably the most common approach. It is also the only one which I recommend you *not* use. I've said "I'll try to do better" in many areas of my life. And, unless I have a specific plan to go with it, the result is always the same. I don't. So, please, keep reading and pick a plan that calls for specific, measurable activity on your part.

Approach #2: Pre-Planned Viewing Blocks

We liked this one. Pre-planned viewing time allowed us to cut back without feeling like we were Robinson Crusoes of the telemedia age. For this, you simply write down which hours the TV will be on (or circle the shows in your *TV Guide*). You might say, "On Mondays, we'll only watch between 8:00 and 9:00 pm; there's nothing worth watching on Tuesdays, etc." Then hold each other accountable and leave the TV off at all other times.

A mom from Minnesota added a clever twist to this in a way that reveals the value of many shows:

> When the *TV Guide* came, my siblings and I would contract
> for the shows we wanted to watch that week. The catch was: We
> could NOT watch any show we had not contracted for, and we
> HAD to watch any show we had signed up for. If something else
> was happening, we had to adhere to our television schedules.
> There's nothing like watching a stupid sitcom when you could be
> doing something more entertaining to dramatize the "costs" of
> television. Soon we were signing up for only our favorite
> programs, and by junior high, we watched almost no TV at all.[1]

Approach #3: Rationed Weekly Tickets

To do this, give everybody in your family, including yourself, a set number of *TV tickets*. (Maybe 10 half-hour tickets per week.) For each half-hour watched, the viewer has to put a ticket into a bowl or piggy-bank. No more tickets this week? No more TV this week! Some parents even give rewards for unused tickets at the end of each week.

Approach #4: Unplug the TV

The basic principle here is that it will take a conscious effort to plug the set in (as opposed to turning it on out of habit). In our case, I had to put one foot on the piano and hoist myself over the TV cabinet to turn it on. The only problem was that I had to unplug it when I was done watching TV. And to do that, I had to put one foot on the piano... Soon Approach #4 had melted away to Approach #1.

Approach #5: No Week-Night TV

Now we're getting serious, because this should also apply *after* the kids go to bed. Experts say it takes about 3 to 4 weeks to work into a new routine or habit, so commit to trying this for that long. Once you've removed from your mind the *possibility* of watching TV on week-nights, you will have removed the *temptation*. In its place you'll find more time for reading, conversation, homework, games, and so on.

Approach #6: Move the TV to a Closet or Basement

This was our last step before we went to the Unimaginable (Approach #7). Our lower-most dwelling space is more of a cellar than a basement. That's where the TVs went for a few months. (If you have a finished basement, it doesn't count. It has to be a place where you wouldn't go to watch even the Superbowl or your favorite soap.)

Approach #7: Get Rid of It

You might want to try Approach #5 or #6 before doing this. It may help you avoid some serious withdrawal symptoms, such as shortness of breath when the evening news would have come on, or sweaty palms in the grocery line next to the *TV Guide* rack.

If you're not sure if you need to do anything about your TV viewing, try a simple test. For the next week, keep a log of how much time you spend face-to-face with your TV and face-to-face with your children. If you are happy with the results—congratulations! If you're not, try one of these approaches soon and decisively.

And don't rule out doing something *rash* with your set. I've talked to dozens of TV-less couples and not one has looked at me with a sad, far-away gaze and sighed, "Oh, for those days of *Laverne and Shirley*." They've all been thrilled with what they could do with the lost hours they've found. Would you get excited if you got a 25% pay raise? Give yourself a 25% time raise. You can always replace the money you've spent. But time, now... that's different. Once you spend it, it's gone.

Chapter 8

Reading: Retaking the High Ground

James loves to read. For as long as he can remember, Mom and Dad have read to him while he lay on the carpet or snuggled in a chair. Their voices would take him to the lower decks of a rolling three-masted schooner, the deepest jungles of India, or faraway worlds that can only be visited in one's imagination. As he became a young reader, his appetite for books was insatiable. His house was filled with rich, full classics and he was often found consuming them in its quietest corners. With each book, his mind grew. Soon he was raising the eyebrows of adults with his word-power, his inquisitive mind, his clear and well-crafted speech. As he became a young man, he sensed the approval of teachers, friends, and employers.

Scott hates to read. Other than the newspaper, he seldom saw his dad read anything. And Mom never read anything to him, except for the riot act when he watched too much TV. He enjoyed video games and sports, but found his school books dry and boring. What's more, reading never came easy, and it seemed to be getting more difficult to "decode" those books with each passing school year. As he grew up, his life was frequented with low test scores, remedial courses, and unrewarding work.

The reality is that there are more Scotts than Jamess today. The tragedy is that it need not be so. With some relatively simple steps (which will be covered in the next chapter), parents can fill their children with a love for reading.

But first, where are we today? Jim Trelease, author of *The Read-Aloud Handbook*, has said, "...in this nation of 42 million children...two out of every three children can't read, won't read, or hate to read."[1]

Can't Read, Won't Read, Hate to Read

For many, reading is not a choice—it's an impossibility. They simply have not been equipped with the skills needed to unlock the world of the written word:

> Sixty million adult Americans cannot read the front page of a newspaper, according to a new report on the problem of illiteracy in the United States by the Northeast Midwest Institute, a non-profit research and education group...
>
> (Rep. Patrick) Williams said many U.S. soldiers cannot use sophisticated weapons because they "can't even begin to read," and the Defense Department spends $1000 a page to convert weapons manuals into comic books for them.[2]

The cost to society is enormous, and it can't be measured in dollars and cents alone. According to Anne Richardson (Chairman of the Board of Reading Is Fundamental, Inc.), 85 percent of the juveniles who appear in court are functionally illiterate.[3]

For many other children, reading is a choice, and they have clearly chosen "no thanks." In 1986, the U.S. Department of Education wrote a pamphlet for parents, *What Works*, in which they described the problem:

...American children do not spend much time reading independently at school or at home. In the average elementary school, for example, children spend just 7 to 8 minutes a day reading silently. At home, half of all fifth graders spend only 4 minutes a day reading.[4]

Compare this to the Soviet Union, in which the average high-school student is assigned at least thirty books per year in his literature courses.[5] Reports show that the number of books actually read is closer to one hundred per year, on average.[6] In fact, *the average Soviet student reads more American and English literature by graduation than does his American counterpart.*[7]

To no one's surprise, the unpopularity of reading is tied to the popularity of television:

A Gallup poll taken during the 1970's showed that 82 percent of the elementary-grade children polled had not read a book in the preceding month, although they each had averaged more than one hundred hours of television during the same period.[8]

These children simply do not realize that reading can be fun! Think back to your childhood. Did you ever take a flashlight with you to bed and read under your covers, because you just couldn't put that book down? Tell that to most kids today and they'll think, "That's wierd!" Many have no concept of reading as a form of entertainment because all they know are dull textbooks and boring basal readers.

Reading vs. Television: Is One Better?

Why am I bemoaning our children's preference for the TV over books? After all, we now live in a brave new world full of computers, video games, and satellite dishes. Perhaps

books are going the way of the buggy whip, and it is only a sense of tradition that causes us to mourn their passing. But I don't think so. Let's compare the two media; we'll forget the generally shabby *content* of television and focus on the *nature* of the two media.

1. Attention Span: With the rapid-fire use of technical shifts, the television viewer's attention is broken into a series of short segments. A good book, however, is designed to hold—not interrupt—the reader's attention. We've seen this in our own home. Whereas our girls will listen to a book for hours, those of their friends with steady TV diets begin some major fidgeting after about 10 or 15 minutes.

2. Pace: When you are watching TV, you are following along at a fixed pace. There's nothing you can do to slow down or speed up the action. With a book, *you* set the pace to match your interest level, your understanding, and your mood.

3. Critical Reaction: For the most part, television's fixed pace turns you into a passive observer. Alpha brain waves take over and you float with the current down the stream coming from your set. With a book, you have time for critical reaction. Sometimes I will slowly absorb a climactic scene line by line, or stop to consider the character's next move, or try to create a picture of the surroundings in my mind.

4. Social Interaction: I can't remember ever seeing TV used as a sparkplug for social interaction. Usually everyone watches in silence, and questions or comments are viewed as rude interruptions. (Speaking of rude, have you ever visited someone who divided his attention between you and a television he couldn't bear to turn off?) Indeed, television is, as T. S. Elliot described, "a medium of entertainment which permits millions of people to listen to the same joke at the same time and yet remain lonely."

Now, reading can be anti-social as well, when the reader gets lost in a different world between the book's covers. But it can also be a special time of closeness and intimacy. It warms me to think of winter evenings with our girls cuddled in our arms, as we read and discussed books. Then, like members of a secret club, we laughed and talked for days about the places we'd visited, the conversations we'd heard, the things we'd seen.

5. Thinking Portrayed: In 1980, the vice president of ABC's children's programming said that many fine children's books could not be adapted for television. He noted that a good portion of the character development found in these books takes place in the character's mind. And, he added, "You simply can't put thinking on the screen."[9]

6. *Imagination:* Both a television program and a book employ the imagination. The difference is that the TV show primarily involves the director's imagination, while the book involves your imagination. When you read Rudyard Kipling's *Rikki-tikki-tavi*, you *are* a mongoose, preparing for a life and death battle with a black king cobra:

> Nag coiled himself down, coil by coil, round the bulge at the bottom of the water jar, and Rikki-tikki stayed still as death. After an hour he began to move, muscle by muscle, toward the jar. Nag was asleep, and Rikki-tikki looked at his big back, wondering which would be the best place for a good hold. "If I don't break his back at the first jump," thought Rikki, "he can still fight. And if he fights—O Rikki!" He looked at the thickness of the neck below the head, but that was too much for him; and a bite near the tail would only make Nag savage.
>
> "It must be the head," he thought at last; "the head above the hood. And, when I am once there, I must not let go."
>
> Then he jumped...[10]

Wouldn't you like to have reading come alive in your home? Wouldn't you prefer to rear a "James" in your home? With the specific steps given in the next chapter you can.

By the way, "James" is a real boy. Last year, over a 12-week period, James Ihde finished reading the 33 books constituting *The Complete Works of Francis Schaeffer*—at the age of 13.

Chapter 9

How to Rear a Lover of Reading

It is a sultry afternoon in Rosser, Tenn., a tiny hamlet near the Tennessee River consisting of one trailer and three dilapidated houses clustered beside a rural state road 120 miles northwest of Nashville. Inside one weathered shack many years past its last paint job, Robert Allen, 35, sits at the supper table. A wood-burning stove stands in one corner. An outhouse in back is hidden deep in snake-infested underbrush. There is a well across the road for drawing water. "A while ago they raised the rent to $20 a month," says Allen, who has lived here with his great-aunt Bevie Jones for the past 21 years. "We used to pay $15."

It could be a hopeless scene, indicative of the worst poverty of rural America. But this musty cabin is the site of a small miracle. As he sits at the table, Allen is engrossed in a copy of Virgil's *Aeneid*, one of the more than 1,000 volumes he has amassed over the years in his personal library, which includes the classics of Greek, European and American literature. Until three years ago this self-taught lover of literature had never set foot in a classroom. "Books were a world to me," says Allen, a gentle, unassuming man with receding hairline and curly red sideburns.[1]

Robert Howard Allen went on to study for his Ph.D. at Nashville's prestigious Vanderbilt University. He had received a full doctoral fellowship after he earned a 3.92 undergraduate grade point average and scored the highest on his Graduate Record Examination. And this by a man who had only eaten at a restaurant once in his entire life, and who wore sweaters held together with safety pins. But this by a man *who loved to read.*

I don't want to deify reading. God never said that He couldn't use illiterate men and women. But look at the examples we have: Jesus, reading in the temple; Paul, whose last recorded request was for Timothy to bring his reading materials; Abe Lincoln, building his mind with a book by candlelight in a log cabin. In fact, can you think of a single influential leader in your life who does not *consume* books and the ideas they contain?

Why rear a "hater of reading" when you can rear a "lover of reading"? I can't tell you that it's easy to do; like most things in life, the blessing seldom precedes the commitment. But I can tell you that it's simple. The following 7 steps are both straightforward and well-proven.

1. Read Aloud

A small mountain of evidence exists today that one of the best (if not *the* best) ways to promote reading is to read aloud to our children. The U.S. Education Department told us this in their report, *Becoming a Nation of Readers: What Parents Can Do*,[2] and they said it again in their booklet, *What Works: Research About Teaching and Learning*.[3] Harlem students who were read to for 20 minutes a day showed "significantly higher gains in vocabulary and comprehension."[4] And the superintendent of Chicago's public schools said, "If we would get our parents to read to their preschool children 15 minutes a day, we could revolutionize the schools."[5]

"When should I start?" you may ask. When did you find out you were expecting a child? Seriously, you really can't start too early. The unborn child can hear your voice when you read aloud—newspapers, a novel, anything—and this soothing sound will be good preparation for the future. As your child begins understanding your words, regularly set aside time for reading aloud those books he will enjoy. Get comfortable, use an expressive voice at an unhurried pace, and take time to ask and answer questions.

2. Be an Example

One mom explains how important it is to be a reading role model for our children to follow:

> When I was growing up, my mother taught by example. Whenever she had a free moment, she would sit down with a book. My brother and I had access to books for as far back as I can remember. We were encouraged to read and to look up words so that we would understand what we were reading.
>
> A few years ago, I began the battle to wean my children away from TV. I threatened, unplugged and punished to no avail. Then I thought of my mom. I had always read in my bedroom or in my study. I began to read in the living room. I frequented second-hand bookstores and brought home all the horse, dog and adventure stories that I had loved as a child. Guess what? My children were fascinated by them. I made time to hear about what and how much they were reading. It became a game to finish a book and then tell the story.
>
> Last week, I realized that the battle had been won. Grandma told my son that he could have anything he wanted for his 14th birthday. Most boys would have asked for a TV, but my son asked for books.[6]

Being an example of a good reader doesn't come easily to most dads. In fact, you'd have to look long and hard to find a species that reads fewer books per year than the average adult American male. But, Dad, your children—especially your sons—look to you for their cues. Over the years, they'll pick up what you pick up, be it a baseball, a Bible, a *TV Guide*, a book.

3. Go Into Training

If you're not a jogger, you won't want to be at the starting line of the next Boston Marathon. If you haven't mastered the "bunny hill" ski slope in Ohio, you'd better not be on the lift to the top of an expert slope in Vail, Colorado. Similarly, if your child's imagination has become numbed in the flickering light of television, it's not wise to start reading *War and Peace* to him for two hours at a time.

If this is your situation, start with shorter books that deal with subjects your child is interested in. Does he have a sports hero? Maybe there's a biography in your library just waiting to be read. Does she think horses are a girl's best friend? You could bring home a good book about a girl and her pony. Then start slowly, reading for short periods and stopping while the interest level is still high. Before long, your child's imagination will grow, much like an exercised muscle, and together you'll be losing yourselves for long stretches in some of the finest classics of literature.

4. Use Phonics to Teach Reading

In a masterful statement of the obvious, the Assistant Education Secretary said, "The surest prevention of illiteracy is making sure kids know how to read."[7]

After decades of raging controversy, the evidence now shows that the best way to do this is with phonics. The U.S.

Education Department concluded:

> Children get a better start in reading if they are taught phonics. Learning phonics helps them to understand the relationship between letters and sounds and to "break the code" that links the words they hear with the words they see in print.
>
> Until the 1930's and 1940's, most American children learned to read by the phonics method, which stresses the relationship between spoken sounds and printed letters. Children learned the letters of the alphabet and the sounds those letters represent. For several decades thereafter, however, the "look-say" approach to reading was dominant: children were taught to identify whole words in the belief that they would make more rapid progress if they identified whole words at a glance, as adults seem to. Recent research indicates that, on the average, children who are taught phonics get off to a better start in learning to read than children who are not taught phonics.[8]

We'll talk about the fascinating history behind the phonics vs. look-say battle when public schools are examined in Chapter 17. The important point is to see that your child begins his reading lessons with phonics. (You can easily do this yourself by using any number of texts, such as Samuel Blumenfeld's *How To Tutor*.[9])

5. Build a Home Library

Mark Twain was well known for the disheveled appearance of his home. A friend once commented on the large number of books scattered about, and the equally striking shortage of bookcases. Twain mused a moment and replied, "Yes, but it's so difficult to get friends to loan you their bookcases."

Don't build your library as Mark Twain did. Buy the books! While it's a great idea to frequent the library and keep a steady stream of books going back and forth, there really is no substitute to building a home library. About 30 years ago, Victor and Mildred Goertzel wrote a book called *Cradles of Eminence.* In it, they described their research of the 400 most eminent people living in this century. They were looking for common factors in the childhoods of these men and women, and a major influence was the home library. They wrote:

> A rule of thumb for predicting success is to know the number of books in the home...[10]

It's a good idea to spread books around your house. What would happen if you put cooky jars full of chocolate chip cookies on your coffee table, by the recliner, on a nightstand? They'd get eaten, right? Try it with some tempting books. You might also consider giving books as presents and reading prizes to your children, letting them build their own libraries.

6. Get the Best

A century ago, Charlotte Mason used the term, "twaddle," to refer to mentally inferior and useless material written for children.[11] More recently, Jim Trelease described about 60% of the 2000 children's books produced annually as "fast food for the mind."[12] You can do better. Much better. Once your child is hooked on reading and being read to, you can introduce him to exciting new worlds that are found in "the great ones." (See Chapter 10.)

I remember lying by the fireplace, with my girls cuddled close, when I began reading *Captains Courageous.* Until my voice gave out three hours later, we were all lost in the world of 19th century cod-fishing on the mighty Atlantic, as a rich spoiled brat, Harvey, grew to be a man.

Do you remember the garden battle of Rikki-tikki-tavi mentioned earlier? I think one reason that *Jungle Book* scene stands out to me is that we had read it under a blanket-covered table with all the lights turned out. As we held that book and flashlight, my young "mongeese" and I were in the world of a dark Indian jungle. We were hooked! C. S. Lewis said:

> A book which is enjoyed only by children is a bad children's story. The good ones last. A book which is not worth reading at age 50 is not worth reading at age 10. [13]

7. Encourage Independent Reading

Recently, a new technique for teaching reading has swept across American schools called SSR (sustained silent reading):

> In a...study made to determine which reading methods "worked," it was shown that among 1,800 Philadelphia fourth-grade students "the more minutes a week of sustained silent reading, the better the pupils achieved."[14]

To simplify the "educationalese," SSR means, "just let the poor kids read to themselves!" (That sounds like something we could do without workbooks, charts, and special classroom materials, doesn't it?) And it really does work. Evidence shows that "the amount of leisure time spent reading is directly related to children's reading comprehension, the size of their vocabularies, and the gains in their reading ability."[15]

You may say, "That's fine, but you don't know my Billy. He's just not going to read to himself without a fight." Maybe he will. Let's say Billy's bedtime is 9:00 PM. You've tucked him in and prayed. Now, just as you're leaving and your finger is on the light switch, you stop, turn around, and say, "You know, Billy, if you want to, you can read this book until 9:15. You don't have to. If you'd rather go to sleep, that's fine too."

I believe if you try this and the other ideas, you're going to have an avid reader on your hands. (We had to set up certain rules in our home, like "Girls, no reading when you're walking up and down the steps.") Once you get them started down the path, there will be no turning back—and in the case of the television, less turning on.

Chapter 10

A Few Favorites

Reading

Dad had seen the car in the factory and fallen in love with it. The affection was entirely one-sided and unrequited. He named it Foolish Carriage because, he said, it was foolish for any man with as many children as he to think he could afford a horseless carriage...

A few days after he bought the car, he brought each of us children up to it, one at a time, raised the hood, and told us to look inside and see if we could find the birdie in the engine. While our backs were turned, he'd tiptoe back to the driver's seat—a jolly Santa Claus in mufti—and pressed down on the horn.

"Kadookah, Kadookah." The horn blaring right in your ear was frightening and you'd jump away in hurt amazement. Dad would laugh until the tears came to his eyes.

"Did you see the birdie? Ho, ho, ho," he'd scream. "I'll bet you jumped six and nine-tenths inches. Ho, ho, ho."

One day, while we were returning from a particularly trying picnic, the engine balked, coughed, spat, and stopped.

Dad was sweaty and sleepy. We children had gotten on his nerves. He ordered us out of the car, which was overheated and steaming. He wrestled with the back seat to get the tools. It was stuck and he kicked it. He took off his coat, rolled up his sleeves, and raised the left-hand side of the hood...

His head and shoulders disappeared into the inside of the hood. You could see his shirt, wet through, sticking to his back.

Nobody noticed Bill. He had crawled into the front seat. And then—"Kadookah. Kadookah."

Dad jumped so high he actually toppled into the engine, leaving his feet dangling in mid-air. His head butted the top of the hood and his right wrist came up against the red-hot exhaust pipe. You could hear the flesh sizzle. Finally he managed to extricate himself. He rubbed his head, and left grease across his forehead. He blew on the burned wrist. He was livid...

Bill, who was six and always in trouble anyway, was the only one with nerve enough to laugh. But it was a nervous laugh at that.

"Did you see the birdie, Daddy?" he asked.[1]

For days, our family laughed about this and other scenes from *Cheaper by the Dozen*. Other books have thrilled us, chilled us, warmed us, and brought tears to our eyes. All have made our lives richer. And all have been *shared* adventures. Like a family scrapbook or slides from a family vacation, these books will carry special memories because we visited the times and places between their covers *together*.

I invite you to build a tradition in your home of reading aloud, not just to encourage reading in your child, but to grow closer and build memories together. For ideas on selecting "the great ones," you can read the following:

The Read-Aloud Handbook by Jim Trelease. Penguin, 1982.
Books Children Love by Elizabeth Wilson. Crossway, 1987.
Honey For a Child's Heart by Gladys Hunt. Zondervan, 1978.

You'll find the first book in even the smallest of public libraries, and the latter two at your local Christian bookstore.

The remainder of this chapter is devoted to giving you a thumbnail sketch of a few of our family's all-time favorites. They've all shown themselves to be good "read-alouds," and they've all been enjoyed by the youngest (age 4-7) and the oldest (early "mid-life"). I'll shirk my responsibility of recommending age levels for each book because a) children of the same age can vary a lot in reading comprehension, b) a child practiced in listening can be challenged by and grow from a book well beyond his supposed reading level, and c) I'd probably do a poor job of it.

Chronicles of Narnia
By C. S. Lewis
1950; Macmillan, 1970.

For most of one winter, our family was spellbound by this classic series. In fact, one of the disappointments in my life is that I'll never be able to read the *Chronicles of Narnia* again for the first time. (This series and *Tales of the Kingdom* are our favorites of the favorites.) In the first book of this Christian allegory, *The Lion, the Witch and the Wardrobe*, four brothers and sisters enter the land of Narnia through an old wardrobe. They find the land under the chilling curse of the White Witch, and together with the beautiful golden lion, Aslan, struggle to free the land from the evil queen's grip. Beautiful allegories, insight into human nature, and thrilling adventure will carry you through centuries of Narnian time in the next six books: *Prince Caspian, The Voyage of the "Dawn Treader," The Silver Chair, The Horse and His Boy, The Magician's Nephew,* and *The Last Battle.* In one scene from the fifth book, the Tisroc—that great and awful ruler of the land of Calormen—was addressed by his children, "To hear is to obey, oh my father and the delight of my eyes; may you live forever." I *liked* that. I thought it would be a good tradition to start in our home, but I was out-voted!

Tales of the Kingdom
By David and Karen Mains
David C. Cook, 1983.

I remember the evening some adult friends came to visit us as Carol was reading this to our girls. To the girls' delight, our friends got hooked, and together we all listened well past their bed-time. The story begins with Scarboy and his younger brother, Little Child, living in Enchanted City—a city awake only at night and ruled by the fire of the evil Enchanter. Together, they escape to Great Park and find The King, whom the Enchanter has said no longer exists. In this and the sequel, *Tales of the Resistance*, you'll meet Caretaker, the Rangers, Princess Amanda, Apprentice Juggler, Pig Girl, the Enchanter's Heralds, and the heart of the resistance—City Taxi Company. Perhaps what moved us the most were the powerful lessons and clear allegory of Christ as King.

Tales From Shakespeare
By Charles and Mary Lamb
Dilithium Press, Ltd., 1986.

I had some serious reservations about reading Shakespeare—with its many twists of plot and varied characters—to young children. But the Lambs, in the early 1800's, masterfully succeeded in condensing and simplifying for children twenty of his tales. While each tale is only 15-20 pages in length, we found both our children and ourselves drawn into the skillfully woven plots. Your family will come to know some of the greatest classics of the English language: *A Midsummer Night's Dream, Much Ado About Nothing, The Merchant of Venice, King Lear, Macbeth, All's Well That Ends Well, The Taming of the Shrew, The Comedy of Errors, Romeo and Juliet, Hamlet,* and others.

Captains Courageous
By Rudyard Kipling
Doubleday and Co., 1897.

This novel, with its nineteenth century sea-faring dialect and terms, will challenge your reading abilities. (I found that I had to do a bit of deciphering as I read to make it more understandable.) But it will be well worth it. Harvey Cheyne, the 15-year old spoiled heir to a railroad magnate, falls overboard his steamship liner and is picked up by the North Atlantic cod-fishing schooner, *We're Here*. The captain, Disko Troop, doesn't believe his tale of riches, and for the first time in his life, Harvey learns the meaning of work. As his callouses grow during the fishing season, he also learns lessons of friendship, reliability, and courage. So will your children, as Harvey emerges from the rolling waves, thundering storms, and thick fogs as a man.

Cheaper by the Dozen
By Frank Gilbreth, Jr. and Ernestine Gilbreth Carey
1948; International Collectors Library.

Your family will roar at the true experiences of the Gilbreth family. Dad was a highly successful efficiency expert just after the turn of this century, who raised 12 children with his wife, Lillie. In addition to the rich humor, there's a real lesson in the stories. Whether Dad was painting Morse code instructions on the walls of their summer lighthouse, playing French records in the bathroom, or using his children to demonstrate his "touch typing system," the message is clear: The home can be an exciting place to learn. Dad believed most adults had stopped thinking: "A child, on the other hand, stays impressionable and eager to learn. Catch one young enough, and there's no limit to what you can teach." (As you read this aloud, you'll want to skip over a handful of expletives.)

Little House in the Big Woods
By Laura Ingalls Wilder
Harper and Row, 1932.

In the "Little House" series, your family will feel like they are living in the American frontierlands of the late 1800's. Laura Ingalls was born in a log cabin at the edge of the Big Woods of Wisconsin. Through the years, she and her family traveled by covered wagon through Kansas, Minnesota, and finally the Dakota Territory, where she met and married Almanzo Wilder. With the best of the American pioneer spirit, the family endured wild animals, hard work, storms, and grasshopper plagues. Yet throughout, they enjoyed Pa's fiddle playing, sleigh rides, socials, and each other. This series also includes: *Little House on the Prairie, Farmer Boy, On the Banks of Plum Creek, By the Shores of Silver Lake, The Long Winter, Little Town on the Prairie, These Happy Golden Years,* and *The First Four Years.*

Robinson Crusoe
By Daniel Defoe
1719; Moody Press, 1965.

From the time of its first publication over 250 years ago, *Robinson Crusoe* has been recognized as one of the great books of all time. We follow the adventures of a young, restless seaman who is cast ashore on an uninhabited tropical island. During the detailed account of his 25 years there, we find ourselves asking how we would go about building a life there with the same scant resources. But make sure you don't get an abridged edition with the best left out, because this is much more than an adventure story. The original edition included many passages revealing the working of the Holy Spirit in his heart, his recognition of his sinful nature, and his acceptance of Christ as his Savior. This, and his constant recognition of God's loving provisions for him—even in the worst of conditions—provide powerful lessons for the reader. While not easy reading, your family will be richly rewarded for the effort.

The Jungle Book
By Rudyard Kipling
1893; Grosset and Dunlap, 1950.

In the seven stories contained in this classic, we meet such animals as Rikki-tikki-tavi, the mongoose; Kotick, the white seal; and Toomai of the Elephants. Our family's favorite character, though, was Mowgli, a baby boy raised by wolves in the jungles of India. On one moon-lit night before the council of wolves, Bagheera, the black panther, paid for the baby's life with a freshly-killed bull. In the coming years, Mowgli owed his life to other friends—Baloo, the old bear and Kaa, the rock python. As he grew in the ways of the jungle, Mowgli eventually overcame that vicious tiger and lifetime enemy, Shere Khan. If your family is completely drawn in as ours was, you'll want to get a copy of *All the Mowgli Stories*, and read how Mowgli grows to be a man and master of the jungle.

Little Women
By Louisa May Alcott
1868; Little, Brown and Co., 1968.

Perhaps no other children's novel has been loved by so many girls as *Little Women*. It is the story of four sisters growing up in the late 1800's. Their father, a gentle minister, is away serving as a chaplain in the Civil War. Although they are poor, they have a loving, dedicated mother to guide them. The girls are very different from each other, and much of the

book's life is drawn from their interaction with each other.
You and your family will quickly become involved with this
lively family, and their lessons of compassion, courage, and
character. If so, you can read the next stories, *Little Men* and
Jo's Boys.

Anne of Green Gables
By Lucy Maud Montgomery
1908; Dilithium Press, 1988.
    This well-loved story is set in a small town on Canada's
beautiful Prince Edward Island. Expecting to pick up an
orphan boy at the train station, Matthew Cuthbert and his
elderly sister, Marilla, instead meet a red-haired, eleven-year-
old girl, Anne Shirley, sent by mistake. "All spirit and fire and
dew," Anne begins changing their stark lives, often in hum-
orous ways. As well as her fantasy, humor, and poetic insight,
she brings her love and her need to be loved.

The Secret Garden
By Frances Hodgson Burnett
1912; J. B. Lippencott Co., 1962.
    Mary Lennox is orphaned in India when her beautiful
mother and her father, a British officer, die suddenly of
cholera. A spoiled, disagreeable child, Mary is sent to
Misselthwaite Manor in England to live with her uncle. There
she meets a kind young servant girl, her nature-loving brother,
and a mysterious invalid boy, Colin, hidden in a remote wing
of the manor. You'll laugh at the scenes when the pampered,
ill-tempered Colin meets his match in fiery, strong-willed
Mary. She also discovers the secret garden which brings
change to all of their lives. (Also by this author: *A Little
Princess.*)

Hans Brinker or The Silver Skates
By Mary Mapes Dodge
1865; Grossett and Dunlap, 1945.

In the preface, the author writes, "Should it cause even one heart to feel a deeper trust in God's goodness and love...the prayer with which it was begun and ended will have been answered." This masterpiece is set in nineteenth-century Holland. Due to a head injury, the father of the Brinker family is mentally afflicted, and has left his family in acute poverty. Both of the children, Hans and Gretel are excellent skaters in the fine Dutch tradition, and many of the most exciting scenes relate to their skill on ice. Ultimately, though, your family will thrill to the displays of courage, faith, loyalty, and love.

Have you seen a common thread running through these selections? It's called *values*. Values you'd like your children to develop. Values they won't pick up from most TV programs. So, you see, when you read the *great* literature (much of it written in days gone by) to your children, your family wins in three ways: 1) Your children develop a love for reading that will serve them well throughout their lives, 2) your family draws together as it shares adventures and builds memories, and 3) your children learn about values—honesty, compassion, faithfulness, bravery—and so much more.

Chapter 11

The Socialization Myth

Peers

"You really should let your child play with others of his age. Otherwise he'll never get socialized."

Have you ever heard these words? They seem to have a ring of truth, yet we wonder: What about our neighbors' child who is bringing home foul language, our friends' 8-year-old who is openly rebelling, those junior high students smoking in the park, the local teens arrested last week? Did they pick up most of their behavior from adults or from other children?

If it seems confusing, I believe it is because the world is confused. For a dose of clear thinking, let's turn to the Bible and find if socialization is recommended.

Is Socialization a Biblical Concept?

First, the definition of the word, socialize, from Webster's New World Dictionary:

> **so-cial-ize** 1. to make social; adjust to or make fit for cooperative group living 2. to adapt or make to *CONFORM* to the common needs of a social group (emphasis added).[1]

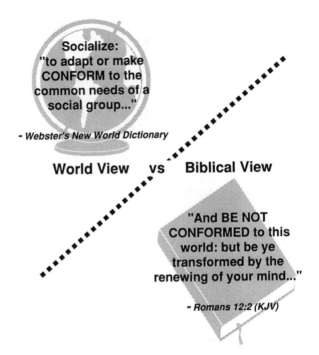

Socialize:
"to adapt or make
CONFORM to the
common needs of a
social group..."

- Webster's New World Dictionary

World View   vs   Biblical View

"And BE NOT
CONFORMED to this
world: but be ye
transformed by the
renewing of your mind..."

- Romans 12:2 (KJV)

Now, a biblical perspective from Romans 12:2:

> And *BE NOT CONFORMED* to this world: but be ye
> transformed by the renewing of your mind, that ye may prove
> what is that good, and acceptable, and perfect will of God
> (emphasis added).[2]

They seem to be in direct contradiction, don't they? For
nearly 2000 years, God's Word has said we should not
conform to the world; now the world says our children should.
And whenever we follow the world's advice instead of God's,
we get into trouble. In this case the trouble is called "the
effects of peer dependency," and will be examined in the next
chapter.

If you looked for the word socialize in older dictionaries,
you wouldn't find it. That's because the word wasn't coined

until earlier this century by some contemporaries of the socialist educator, John Dewey.

These socialists didn't see each truth as an absolute, but rather as a universal, commonly held belief. They believed a process (called Hegelian) took place among people by which truth was continually becoming purer and purer. In this process a group belief (thesis) was challenged by an opposing belief (antithesis) and the ensuing conflict led to a compromise (synthesis). The process would rely heavily on people interacting with each other, hence the need to prepare the child through socialization.

The danger of socialization without absolute values can be made clear through an example: Suppose you met a member of the Crips, a Los Angeles street gang so named for its practice of crippling its victims. Is that gang member socialized? Sure he is. He is conforming to the common needs of his social group! But he is doing so without some important *absolute* values.

What Do Your Friends Mean by Socialization?

Let's be fair. When your friends say your child should be socialized, they probably aren't thinking you should oversee the making of a socialist or a street gang member. Instead, the idea is to teach your child to be nice and share his toys, right?

I know it's simplistic, but I believe many people have an abstract picture of the socialization process that looks something like Figure 11.1. I did. First you start with an unsocialized child. Maybe you've seen one. (Maybe you have one!) This child is then thrust into the company of other little children. Now, we don't know what those children are saying or doing. We don't know what's going on in this "black box." We just know that our children are getting... well, you know... socialized.

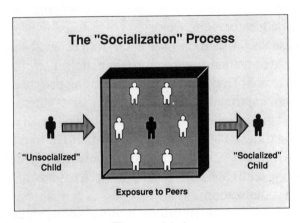

Figure 11.1

Let's think about this. Carol and I spent months teaching our daughters that baby spoons were eating utensils, not catapults. Just before Velcro made them obsolete, we painstakingly taught them how to tie their shoe laces. Together, we felt excitement as we put away the changing table, the training wheels, and the water wings, because *we* had taught them.

And when it's time to teach one of life's most important lessons—how to build caring relationships with others—WHO should teach them? An untrained child? You mean like that one? The one pulling the cat's tail? I think we need another dose of clear thinking. We'd better turn to a best-seller on child-rearing. In it we learn that:

> Folly is bound up in the heart of a child... (Proverbs 22:15)[3]

While this may not sound kind, we are being told that children are, by nature, foolish. The Bible goes on to say:

> He who walks with the wise grows wise, but a companion of fools suffers harm. (Proverbs 13:20)[4]

So children are foolish, and companions of the foolish suffer harm. It doesn't sound like we ought to turn over the teaching of important lessons to our children's playmates.

The Modeling Process

In place of the "black box" illustration, it's been helpful for me to think in terms of the modeling process shown in Figure 11.2. In this process, the child is exposed to both adults and other children. After a childhood full of such exposure, the child enters young adulthood with behavior that falls somewhere in the range between good and bad.

Now here is a simple generalization: The more a child is exposed to other children, the worse that child's behavior will be; the more a child is exposed to adults (especially loving parents), the better the behavior. There are exceptions to this, of course, but you'll see quite a bit of support for this generalization in the next chapter.

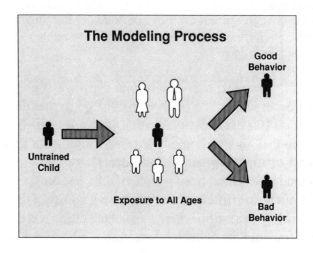

Figure 11.2

So what do we do at the Adams home when we see some neighborhood children coming down the sidewalk? Quickly, we grab the girls in from the porch, slam the front door, and hide them in the closet... Well, not exactly. Actually, we try to do two things. First, we try to spend some time with them in the "black box" to help our girls *and* their friends understand important lessons of kindness, compassion, helpfulness, etc. (more on this later). The second is to expose our girls to people of all ages, not just their own.

The latter approach is called *age-integration* instead of *age-segregation*. Age-integration has been practiced from the beginning of society until the beginning of this century. Children grew up playing with brothers and sisters and other children of all ages. They also were heavily influenced by aunts and uncles, older cousins, grandmas and grandpas, and of course, Mom and Dad. As Urie Bronfenbrenner recalls, even the neighbors played a role:

> If you walked on the railroad trestle, the phone would ring at your house, and your parents would know what you had done before you got back home. People on the street would tell you to button your jacket, and ask why you were not in church last Sunday. Sometimes you liked it and sometimes you didn't—but at least people *cared*.[5]

Today, however, our society practices age-segregation. Here's how it works: "You 3-year-olds; go to that day-care center. You 10-year-olds; over in that 4th grade. All you older folks; into that nursing home." (Are we training our children to institutionalize us when we're older?)

Instead of learning from people of all ages, most children are now put in an artificial environment with those of the same age. They live in a world where most of the citizens were born within a few months of each other. And it's having a strange effect on their behavior... as we shall see in the next chapter.

Chapter 12

The Effects of Peer Dependency

The father of a teen-age girl had finally heard enough of her butchered English. He took her aside and said, "You've got to quit using two words in particular. One is gross and the other is awesome."

"For sure, Dad," his daughter replied, "What are they?"

Have you ever talked with a teen and found "it's like, you know, totally, like, hard to even, like, understand each other?" If you *did* understand each other, you may have found that the differences ran deeper than dialect.

Certainly it is normal for teens and their parents to struggle a bit as youngsters test their wings and prepare for solo flight. But how many of today's parent/teen problems are natural, and how many of them are evidence of excessive peer dependency? Since World War II, the problem has grown so large that we have given it a name—the generation gap.

We'll wait until Chapter 13 to discuss the causes for this gap. For now, let's look at what happens when children begin heavily orienting and identifying with other children. Let's look at seven negative effects of peer dependency.

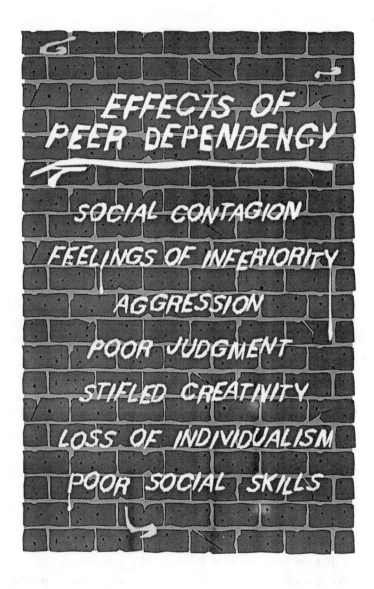

Effect #1: Social Contagion

If *social contagion* is a new term for you, picture this: You are an invisible passenger sitting in the back of a school bus, surrounded by 6th-grade boys. Social contagion is what you are watching and hearing:[1]

> habits
> manners
> finger signs
> obscenities
> rivalry
> ridicule

In short, this is behavior that you would not teach your child, but that some other children would be only too happy to teach him. After I gave this example in one seminar, I was corrected by a father who said, "That's happening long before 6th grade. Last year our son went to kindergarten, and by Thanksgiving, he was bringing home language that I had to explain to my wife!"

Effect #2: Feelings of Inferiority

Today, folks often equate adolescence with low self-esteem. Our hearts ache as we read how children, mired in poor self-images, use drugs, alcohol, and suicide to self-destruct. But is this natural or is it a result of the age-segregated world in which children now live? Psychologist and author Dr. James Dobson concludes:

> ...the epidemic of inferiority and inadequacy seen during the teen years is rooted in the ridicule, rejection, and social compet-ition experienced by vulnerable young children. They are simply not ready to handle the threats to the self-concept that are

common in any elementary school setting.

I have seen kids dismantle one another, while parents and teachers passively stood by and observed the "socialization" process. I've then watched the recipients of this pressure begin to develop defense mechanisms and coping strategies that should never be necessary in a young child.[2]

Effect #3: Aggression and Delinquency

In the Soviet Union, many children were orphaned during the communist revolution. In the early 1920's, bands of these orphans roamed about and were notorious for their acts of selfishness, callousness, and violence.[3] At first, I saw this as a unique example of age-segregation leading to violence. Then I realized it wasn't unique at all. In every major U.S. city we have the modern-day equivalent—street gangs—where a child's family becomes other children and his lifestyle becomes violence.

The problem doesn't start when a child hits his teen years. It starts when he hits a roomful of other children, and spends a good part of his day there. Writer Dale Farran describes the results of one day-care study:

> In another day-care study at a child-development center, children who started in day care at the age of six weeks and continued until age five were compared with a control group who had been in home care or gone to day care at a later age. When the first section of the experimental group was measured for aggression, they were found to be *fifteen* times as aggressive as the controls.[4] (Italics mine)

These long-term day-care residents were also found to be more easily frustrated, less cooperative, more distractable, and less task-oriented.

Effect #4: Poor Judgment and Foolishness

When a group of inexperienced peers looks to itself for direction, poor judgment often results. We have a prime example of this from scripture: When Solomon was king, he had an impressive building program. He also had an impressive national budget which was financed by a source familiar to the average taxpayer—the peoples' pockets.

When Solomon died and his son Rehoboam took over, these people asked for some relief. We pick up the story at I Kings 12:6-8:

> Then King Rehoboam consulted the elders who had served his father Solomon during his lifetime. "How would you advise me to answer these people?" he asked.
> They replied, "If today you will be a servant to these people and serve them and give them a favorable answer, they will always be your servants."
> But Rehoboam rejected the advice the elders gave him and consulted the young men who had grown up with him and were serving him.[5]

Rehoboam took the advice of his young friends and told the people, "My little finger is thicker than my father's waist." (A tenth-century-B.C. expression for, "You ain't seen nothing yet!") As a result, Israel split permanently from Judah. All because a young man made a foolish decision based on the advice of his peer group.

Today, our newspapers are full of similar tragedies. Look behind the story of the vandalized school, the high-speed car accident, the gang rape. More often than not, you'll find the foolish advice of a peer group.

Effect #5: Stifled Creativity

When the Goertzel's did their study of eminent men and women, they found a lot of creativity. They saw people who had the confidence needed to break out of the mold and apply some unfettered, creative thinking.   Unfortunately, the Goertzel's have seen a more recent trend away from such thinking among our age-segregated youth:

> In what anthropologists tell us is the most peer-oriented culture in the world, the child becomes almost afraid to think until he learns what his classmates are thinking.[6]

Effect #6: Loss of Individualism

Closely related to the loss of creativity is the loss of individualism. Now, I'm not talking about Frank Sinatra's *I-Did-It-My-Way* type of individualism. I'm talking about a young man or lady who is not afraid to stand up for what he believes in front of his peers. A *God-pleaser*, not a *man-pleaser*.

It should not surprise us that our "socialized" children are losing their individualism. After all, somebody who is conforming to the common needs of his social group *must* lose his individualism. What's disturbing is that children don't seem to lose this chameleon-like behavior as they pass into adulthood. Everywhere I look there are signs of adult conformity— in our dress, in our speech, in our ideas. I even have a hunch the growing popularity of opinion polls is an unconscious desire by many to make sure they're not out of step with mainstream America.

Have you ever thought of your child and imagined what type of contribution he'll someday make? The young missionary, political leader, or philosopher is certainly one who has learned to weigh—not count—his critics. Although I don't subscribe to some of his thinking, I believe George Bernard Shaw offered good insight on the subject:

> The reasonable man adapts himself to the world; the unreasonable man persists in trying to adapt the world to himself. Therefore, all progress depends on the unreasonable man.

Effect #7: Poor Social Skills

In our family, we limit unsupervised peer interaction for the very reason many promote it. That is, Carol and I have found that *we* need to be involved to promote social skills—sharing, compassion, cooperation, tolerance, love.

Carol first saw this need when the girls were still quite young: When she was in the same room with our daughters and several of their friends, they had a fairly high standard of behavior. The children's tone of voice, choice of words, and overall attitude seemed to be good. When Carol was in the room next to where the girls were playing, she noticed that their behavior slipped a notch or two. And when they played in the driveway (and she could hear them through an open window), they would spend much more time arguing, teasing, and generally having a hard time getting along.

So Carol started a weekly get-together for the girls which she called the "Friendship Club." Each week they would learn a Bible verse and have a fun activity. (If you have never seen seven little girls making seven little apple pies or seven little pine cone wreaths at the same time, you have no idea what a saint my wife is.)

The main focus of the club—in their verses, their lessons, their weekly interaction—was to learn how to get along with each other. Often Carol would pin a little bag to each girl's shirt, containing colored beads. If Julie said something unkind to Becky, Julie would have to give Becky one of her red beads. If Julie was out of beads 20 minutes into the club time, you knew she was having a bad day!

The point is it worked. None of the girls has said an unkind word since we started the club. OK, so it didn't work *that* well. But, over a period of two years, we saw an improvement. They didn't just teach each other, though. They needed help. They needed adults.

After reading of all the evils of peer dependency, you might feel discouraged. Please don't! I believe that if we understand how children become peer dependent, we can do a lot to prevent it. To Chapter 13, then, for the cause and prevention of peer dependency.

Chapter 13

The Cause and Prevention
of Peer Dependency

"Jimmy, why did you fill up your sister's dollhouse with sand?"

"I dunno."

"Was Bobby showing you how to play with your dump truck again?"

"I dunno."

"What do you mean you don't know? Were you *there*? You weren't unconscious while you were pouring sand down the chimney, were you?"

"I guess not."

"Well, I know you can be nicer than that. Besides, you don't want to do everything your friends say, do you?"

"I dunno."

Perhaps you've seen some effects of peer dependency beginning to show up in your child's behavior. Or maybe you've just recognized these effects in other children and thought, "We don't need *that*." But how do you stop it? To prevent the effects of peer dependency, we must understand

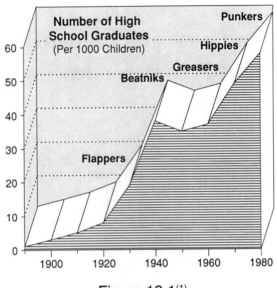

Figure 13.1[1]

its cause. And there is a two-part answer to the question, "What causes peer dependency?" First, *peer dependency results when a child spends too much time with his peers.*

I believe we can see this on a national level over the last century. As shown in Figure 13.1[1], the number of children attending high school has mushroomed. (In 1890, a community with 1000 children would graduate less than 2 per year; today nearly 60 would graduate annually.) The early 20th century marked the first time in our country's history that droves of children were segregated with their age-mates until young adulthood. It also marked the first time that peer-dependent fads began appearing every 10 to 20 years—flappers, beatniks, greasers, hippies, and punkers. While this doesn't prove a cause-and-effect relationship, there seems to be a link between age-segregation and peer-dependency.

On a smaller scale, some studies show a relationship between excessive time with peers and peer dependency. In one study, pre-school children who spent the most time together (in a daycare setting) were also the most peer-oriented.[2]

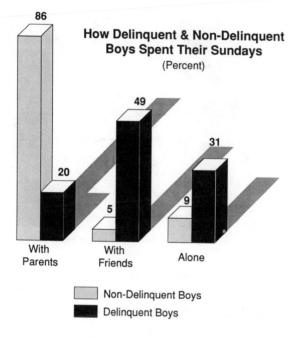

Figure 13.2[3]

In another study, researchers examined the lifestyles and behaviors of delinquent and non-delinquent English boys (Figure 13.2).[3] A high percentage of the delinquent boys spent their free time with other boys. The vast majority of non-delinquent boys, however, spent this time with their parents.

But Why So Much Time With Peers?

Children become peer-dependent because they spend a lot of time together. That's good to know, but the pressing question then becomes: *"Why do they spend a lot of time together?"*

Bronfenbrenner, Condry, and Siman conducted a study of 766 sixth-grade children which answers this question.[4] The

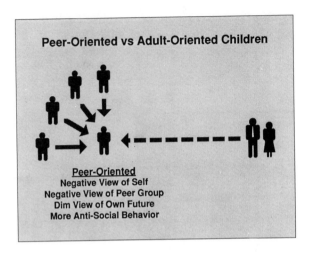

peer-oriented children showed the typical symptoms—a negative view of self and peer group, a dim view of their own future, and antisocial behavior (such as breaking the law, playing "hooky," lying, teasing, etc.)

Then the researchers asked the million-dollar question: "How did the peer-oriented children get that way?" Did the parents *push* their children toward the peer group or did the peer group *pull* the children toward it? Bronfenbrenner reported:

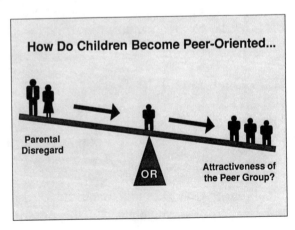

An analysis of data on the child's perception of his parents, his peers, and himself *led us to conclude that the "peer-oriented" youngster was more influenced by a lack of attention and concern at home than by the attractiveness of the peer group.* (Italics mine)

...Their parents were rated as lower than those of the adult-oriented children both in the expression of affection and support, and in the exercise of discipline and control.

...In summary, it would seem that the peer-oriented child is more a product of parental disregard than of the attractiveness of the peer group—that he turns to his age-mates less by choice than by default. The vacuum left by the withdrawal of parents and adults from the lives of children is filled with an undesired —and possibly *undesirable*—substitute of an age-segregated peer group.[5]

What Can We Do About It?

Every time I read this conclusion, I feel a great sense of responsibility. It tells me that Carol and I are our daughters' first choice. If they spend most of their free time with other children, it's probably because their first choice was too busy, and they had to settle for their second choice. Sadly, if parents forfeit this position too often for too long, they lose it... perhaps forever. So what can you do as a parent to stay close to your children, and prevent them from falling into the trap of peer dependency?

1) Limit peer interaction to a *reasonable* level. Be especially careful not to turn your very young child loose among age-mates for long periods of time. From a study of children in daycare (Figure 13.3), it became clear that *younger* children do the most imitation, and that of peers more than adults.[6]

2) Don't be a stranger to your child's friends. Get to know them and look for fun things you can all do together. And when they are younger, you can actively guide them toward improving the way they interact with each other. Carol has

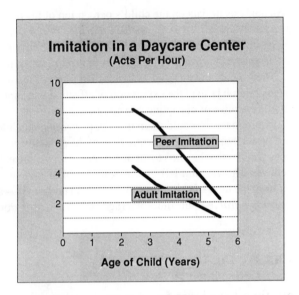

Figure 13.3[6]

spent many a day acting as supervisor and referee, counselor and confidante. Not an easy job, but worthwhile.

3) Plan age-integrated activities. Look for ways to get your children involved with folks of all ages. Next time friends come, why not plan an activity for everyone, instead of sending all the kids to the basement while the adults visit?

4) Stay in touch with your child's thoughts. In today's fast-paced world, it's so easy to stop talking (I mean *really* talking) with those living under the same roof. As a result, many children have left the world of "Father knows best" and entered the world of "I'll ask the guys." (Figure 13.4[7]: Note that this trend has been particularly severe among teen-age girls.)

5) Be fun to be with! I don't think it would be inappropriate for you to think of yourself as being in competition with TV and peers for your child's attention. Like any other relationship, it's not realistic to think you can build a solid, lasting one without putting something of yourself into it.

Where Teens Go For Advice...

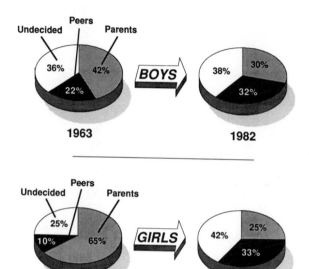

Figure 13.4[7]

The good news is that *you* are going to have more fun if you break out of the rat race and begin enjoying your children. There will be some difficult times during those teen years. And, yes, as they grow up, they will be spending more time outside your family. But by building a strong family root system when your children are young—and then nurturing it—your family bonds will endure, even thrive.

Chapter 14

What Pulls Parents
From Their Children?

John Henry Fabre, the great French naturalist, conducted a most unusual experiment with some Processionary Caterpillars. These caterpillars blindly follow the one in front of them. Hence, the name. Fabre carefully arranged them in a circle around the rim of a flower pot, so that the lead caterpillar actually touched the last one, making a complete circle. In the center of the flower pot he put pine needles, which is food for the Processionary Caterpillar. The caterpillars started around this circular flower pot. Around and around they went, hour after hour, day after day, night after night. For seven full days and seven full nights they went around the flower pot. Finally, they dropped dead of starvation and exhaustion. With an abundance of food less than six inches away, they literally starved to death...[1]

What are you chasing? Are you relentlessly pursuing something that doesn't allow you the time to turn aside to your children who are just "inches" away? Do you, like the processionary caterpillar, chase out of habit, not stopping to think about what you are missing, or even what you are chasing?

I feel convicted by my own questions. I believe many of us are products of our own culture, locked in a hectic routine. Faster and faster we go, like kids on a merry-go-round gone wild. We get fast money from the automatic teller. Fast food from the microwave. Fast mail from Federal Express. Fast news from the TV. Fast travel from the freeway. Fast debt from the shopping mall. Yet, for all this blinding speed, we don't have more time to relax, to invest in relationships—we have less.

We are like 33 rpm records that are being played at 45 rpm. We sound like those chipmunks, Alvin, Simon, and Theodore, but we don't notice anymore. And we don't know how to turn the speed back down. So we just keep packing in more and more.

Have you ever heard someone say, "Yup, things are pretty slow around our place. You know, not too much going on in the evenings. Plenty of time to sit on the porch, visit with the neighbors, play with the kids. That sort of thing"? Me neither.

You'll note that this chapter is titled, "What Pulls Parents From Their Children?" and not "What Pulls Children From Their Parents?" I know it looks like the TV and the peer group are pulling our kids away from us. But those are just symptoms. It's all after the fact—*we* moved first. The root problem is that we have pulled away from our children, often because we're too busy chasing other things. So what are we chasing?

What Are We Chasing?

I had a good chuckle when I saw this bumper sticker: "The Man Who Dies With The Most Toys Wins." Then I started thinking about some fellows I know, and I realized that for them it wasn't a joke—it was a way of life.

In many ways this chasing comes from peer pressure. The boy who just has to have the shirt with the alligator on it

becomes the teen who has to have the fast, shiny, sports car. He grows up to become a man who has to have a large house, or that corner office. Or maybe he's still trying for the fast shiny sports car.

It's not necessarily wrong to acquire these things, but there is a price that must be paid for them. We think we pay with dollars, but the *real* currency is usually hours. Unlike money, time can never be replaced after it is spent. If you worked late to get the promotion to get the boat when Kelly was five, you can always sell the boat and get most of your money back. But Kelly is now nine, and *for the rest of your life—and hers—she'll never be five again.*

It's not just Dad or Mom who pay. Remember the study mentioned earlier, in which almost half of the children said they liked TV better than Dad?[2] That's because the average 5-year-old spends one *minute* in close interaction with Dad for every *hour* he spends with the TV![3] If Dad is too busy buying something, his little guy or his little girl is paying for it.

I don't mean to suggest that the problem begins and ends with Dad. Since World War II, mothers have entered the workforce in unprecedented numbers (Figure 14.1[4]). It's not

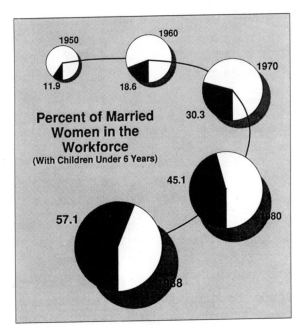

Figure 14.1[4]

my place to say whether or not any woman should go to work outside the home. For many couples in our economy today, it's really not a matter of choice. But I would be doing a terrible disservice if I didn't say that the price our young children pay for Mom working is far greater than most parents have been led to believe. (In the next chapter, we'll explore this further.)

What Is Chasing Us?

It's not just the things we chase that send our schedules into a tailspin. It's also the things that chase us. Like those caterpillars being pushed from behind, many of us have a knack for over-committing ourselves.

All across this country, moms are hurting from a lifestyle Dr. James Dobson has labeled "routine panic." He conducted an inquiry among middle-class married women, between 25 and 35 years of age:

> I asked them to indicate the sources of depression which most often sent them into despair and gloom. Many common problems were revealed, including in-law conflicts, financial hardships, difficulties with children, sexual problems, and mood fluctuations associated with menstrual and physiological distress. But to my surprise, *fatigue and time pressure* was tagged as *the* most troublesome source of depression by half the group; the other half ranked it a close second!...Why do they do it? The women whom I surveyed admitted their dislike for the pace they kept, yet it has become a monster which defies containment.[5]

Many of the things we commit our time to are very good, but if you are *over-committed* to anything else, you are *under-committed* to your family. You don't have to drop everything and move to the mountains to make time for your child. You

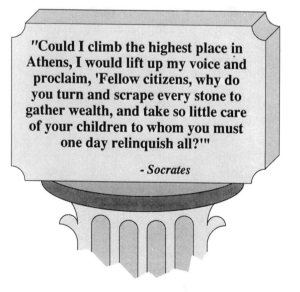

"Could I climb the highest place in Athens, I would lift up my voice and proclaim, 'Fellow citizens, why do you turn and scrape every stone to gather wealth, and take so little care of your children to whom you must one day relinquish all?'"

- Socrates

do have to consider if your child can afford what will be taken from him before you say, "Sure, I'll help."

Getting Off the Flower Pot

Let's think about getting off the rim of the flower pot and getting to the pine needles. To those caterpillars busy chasing, I've got bad news: You really can't *have* it all (regardless of what the ads say.) And for those caterpillars being chased: You really can't *do* it all. If we want to stop chasing and being chased, we're going to have to break out of the high-speed, post-World-War II lifestyle. We'll need to march to the beat of a different drum.

If I stop playing my tape on fast-forward, and begin playing it at the speed the Sound Engineer created it for, I may sound a little odd to those used to hearing only fast-forward. Co-workers might be surprised that my heart isn't set on driving only late-model cars, and someone might be disappointed when I don't volunteer for a worthy cause. But I know a few people who will love the pace—I'm married to one and the others call me Daddy.

Chapter 15

Why Children Need
Their Parents' Time

Jeremy stepped down from the speakers' platform after giving his address to the graduation class. He had felt as nervous as a "long-tailed cat in a room full of rocking chairs," but now he was again glad to have been the class president that year... Deborah pushed her pencil and entrance exam away and leaned back. She was tired, but inside she knew she had "nailed it"... Jessica finished her routine with an impressive leap and a graceful tour en l'air. She waited behind the curtains for her smiling parents to join her.

What do these young adults have in common? *Parents who spent quantity time with them.* Leadership, achievement, strong mental development, high self-esteem, social maturity, peer independence—according to the research, such are the fruits of strong parent-child bonds. While less fortunate children can develop these qualities, the evidence shows the scales are tipped heavily in favor of the child whose parents invest plenty of time in him or her. Let's look more closely at some of these characteristics and how they are promoted.

Mental Development

Decades ago a remarkable study of mentally retarded, institutionalized, three-year-old children was begun by Harold Skeels.[1] A control group was left in the institution and 13 of the children (the experimental group) were taken out. These 13 were placed in the care of mentally retarded women at another state institution, one child per woman. Each of these "mothers" in the institution spent a large amount of time with "her child," playing, talking, and training. The children received non-stop attention and gifts; they were taken on trips, and were exposed to all kinds of special opportunities.[2]

That was the setting. Now let's look at the results, reported by Bronfenbrenner:

> During the formal experimental period, which averaged a year and a half, the experimental group showed a gain in IQ of 28 points (from 64 to 92), whereas the control group dropped 26 points. Upon completion of the experiment, it became possible to place the institutionally-mothered children in legal adoption. Thirty years later, all 13 children in the experimental group were found to be self-supporting, all but two had completed high school, with four having one or more years of college. In the control group, all were either dead or still institutionalized.[3]

Just think of the impact those mentally retarded "moms" had on their children! Think of the impact we can have on our children if we'll just spend the time with them. It breaks my heart when I hear well-meaning parents talk of sending their children to pre-school so they can get a "head start." What their children need most is love and nurture and attention, and they'll have all the "head start" they will ever need.

This was clearly shown in another classic study, this time with Ugandan children in the 1950's.[4] Two groups of young children were compared: those reared in the African tradition and those reared the emerging European way. For the first two years of infancy, the mothers of the first group centered their whole interest on their children. These mothers never left them, carried them on their backs, and constantly played with and stimulated their children. With the new European methods, children in the second group were typically left with nannies and nurseries. These children were often bottle-fed and passed "most of their lives in cots and fed at regular intervals."[5] The researcher, Marcelle Geber, found the African-reared children to be much more advanced in motor development, language, adaptivity, and personal-social relations.

More recent work tells us why this was so. Dr. Richard Restak, one of the world's foremost authorities on the human brain, reports that cell growth in one section of an infant's brain is actually stimulated by snuggling, rocking, and cuddling:

> When an infant is rocked or cuddled, impulses are directed to the cerebellum that stimulate its development, a process that goes on until at least age two. In fact, the cerebellum is unique, since it is the only part of the brain where brain-cell multiplication continues long after birth.[6]

Restak concludes:

> Physical holding and carrying of the infant turns out to be the most important factor responsible for the infant's normal mental and social development.[7]

Social Development

As more and more women have entered the workforce, and more children have been placed in day-care, research has begun to pile up regarding the effects of day-care on those children. The news is not good. In the 1970's, Jay Belsky (child psychologist, Pennsylvania State University) was viewed as a leading defender of full-time day care. He has since reversed his position, citing recent research which shows a high rate of insecurity for day-cared children under 18 months (with behavior adversely affected until at least ages 9 and 10).[8]

Dr. Burton White, a renowned psychologist and former director of the Harvard Preschool Project, said:

> Put simply, after more than 20 years of research on how children develop well, I would not think of putting a child of my own into any substitute care program on a full-time basis, especially a center-based program.[9]

Why all the doomsaying? Much of it has to do with *attachment* or *bonding*. Experts are increasingly recognizing the need for infants to form a strong bond of trust with at least one loving, caring adult, especially during the first year of life. Some researchers have gone so far as to link the behavior of psychopathic mass murderers to an absence of bonding during their infancy.[10]

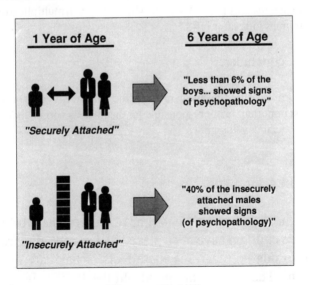

Figure 15.1[(11)]

Closer to home has been a study of boys as they grew from one to six years of age (Figure 15.1[11]). Researchers found that less than 6% of the boys who had been classified as securely attached at age one showed signs of psychopathology at six years. (Psychopathology is amoral or asocial behavior characterized by irresponsibility and lack of remorse.) Forty percent of the insecurely attached boys, however, showed such signs at age six. In reviewing the results, Drs. Gamble and Zigler concluded:

> Overall results suggest that, as a matter of sound public policy, alternatives to day care be made available to families with infants.[12]

So what are these alternatives, you ask? Some parents would love to have Mom stay home, but they just can't make ends meet. For them it's not a matter of doing without a late model car or bigger house—it's a matter of putting food on their table, clothes on their backs, and a roof over their heads. My heart especially goes out to single parents who face enormous obstacles in meeting their families' emotional and financial needs. Here are some suggestions to help make the best of the situation:

1) Arrange to have a relative, close friend, or neighbor take care of your child in their home. The key is to make the care as close as possible to what you would provide—with love, nurturing, and a non-institutional, home-like atmosphere.

2) In two-parent homes, stagger your working hours if possible, so one parent will be home with the child. If you can't totally eliminate full-time care, try to shorten the hours by selecting a care-giver close to your job or by staggering your work hours slightly.

3) If your child is cared for by someone else during the day, make sure you spend a lot of "carpet time" with your youngster in the evening to build a strong bond.

4) Do whatever you can to keep your child out of a day-care center for at least the critical first two years of your child's life.

Most of the above work deals with very young children. But research shows that our children also need time with us as they get older. This time is so important, that without it, some turn to crime! In a study of delinquent and non-delinquent boys, the non-delinquent boys frequently helped their mother and shared hobbies with their father (Figure 15.2[13]). In contrast, the delinquent boys seemed to be crying out that they were not getting enough of their parents—especially Dad.

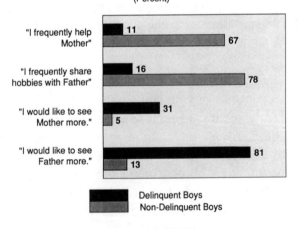

Response of Delinquent & Non-Delinquent Boys
(Percent)

"I frequently help Mother" 11 67

"I frequently share hobbies with Father" 16 78

"I would like to see Mother more." 31 5

"I would like to see Father more." 81 13

Delinquent Boys
Non-Delinquent Boys

Figure 15.2[13]

Parent/Child Understanding

In a recent study, parents were asked to guess their college-age children's views in eight different subjects.[14] The children had been asked for their opinions on a series of questions concerning the family, religion, U.S. foreign involvement, drugs, marriage, maternal employment, sexual permissiveness, and the work ethic. Parents made the best guesses in the areas of fundamentalist religious beliefs and sexual permissiveness, but overall showed a very limited knowledge of what their children thought about important issues.

Compare their knowledge of their offspring to that of Jane Goddall, a young British scientist who spent years observing chimpanzees in Africa. She invested hundreds of painstaking hours watching, studying, and compiling data on them.[15] After reading an account of this work, Jean Fleming (author of *A Mother's Heart*) asked, "I wonder if Jane Goddall knows her monkeys better than I know mine?"[16] It's a question many of us probably should ask ourselves, because strong life-long relationships are built on understanding. And that takes time.

Strong Character Development

The research tells us that a number of positive character qualities are fostered when parents are involved with their children. Several studies show this by examining a worst-case scenario—that in which a parent is absent. Studies have explored the effects of father absence in the following settings: middle-class American adolescents,[17,18] soldiers' families during World War II,[19] homes of Norwegian sailors and whalers,[20] and households in the West Indies.[21] Taken together, this work points to the following attributes developed in children without a father:

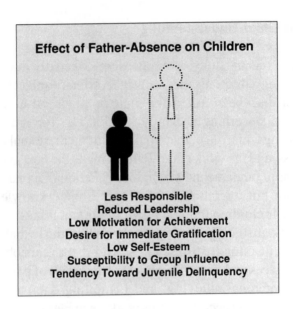

Effect of Father-Absence on Children

Less Responsible
Reduced Leadership
Low Motivation for Achievement
Desire for Immediate Gratification
Low Self-Esteem
Susceptibility to Group Influence
Tendency Toward Juvenile Delinquency

If we know that this is the fruit of a fatherless home, then we know the dangers of a home in which the parents both live, but don't spend much time with their child. And knowing this encourages us to apply the antidote—or more accurately, the vaccine—*time with our children*. Practical ideas on how to do this is what the next chapter is all about.

Chapter 16
Principles for Parent-Child Time

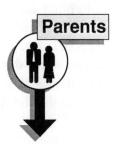

Let's say you're driving home from work and the kids are waiting for you. You've been giving it some thought and, by golly, things are going to be different around your house from now on. You're going to cut back on that TV. And you've got ideas on how to wrap up some of your own time commitments and begin committing more time to your own flesh and blood.

The truth is, if you spend more time doing practically anything with your children, your family will benefit. But there are some principles you can apply when you are with your children which will make the time even richer, more valuable, more exciting. We'll look now at nine principles.

Principle #1: Touch Your Child's Palate

Proverbs 22:6, perhaps the most quoted verse on child-rearing, instructs us to "train up a child in the way he should go and, when he is old, he will not depart from it."[1] According to Charles Swindoll, the original root word for "train up" is the term for the palate, the roof of the mouth, the gums.[2] In a beautiful illustration put forth by Gregg Harris, we see the young Hebrew mother taking a morsel of food that she has chewed out of her mouth, and lightly touching it to the palate of her baby.[3]

That which was delighting her palate will, over time, begin to delight the palate of her child. Her tastes will become her child's tastes. What is delighting your palate? What are you chewing on which you could share with your child, by example or by occasional discussions—but not by "preaching" to him? You'll note that the Hebrew mom did not take a whole mouthful and "cram" it down her child's throat; she "touched" his palate. A few possibilities:

> Reliance upon God's Word
> Desire to Share Christ
> Love of Reading
> Prayer
> Compassion
> Enjoyment of Music
> Appreciation for Nature
> Sense of Humor
> Thirst for Learning
> Good Taste

I enjoy listening to classical music, so I play it frequently in our home. Guess what? Our girls enjoy it, too. We also enjoy bluegrass music (which may sound like quite a paradox), so we're learning to play guitar, mountain and hammered dulcimers, and violin (also spelled f-i-d-d-l-e). "Wait a minute!" you might say, "What right do you have to force your tastes on your children?" And I'll agree that we have to be careful not to cram the mouthful down. But, to put it bluntly, God gave *us* the baby spoons. If we choose not to use those spoons, someone may come along and offer them something we might not. We wouldn't let a stranger feed our toddler Twinkies and beer. In the same way, I don't want my daughters' first taste of music to be a heavy metal concert at the stadium. They will ultimately choose their musical preferences, but at least they'll have something with which to compare.

The last item on the list is "good taste." As we bring up three daughters, we're trying to teach them how to dress in a charming, attractive, and ladylike fashion. Then maybe, just maybe, when they're 16, they won't want to get orange mohawks. (Such are the things parents strive for!)

A final word on touching your child's palate. *You* have to be chewing something before you can touch your child's palate with it. Often children rebel against their parents' faith because they don't see Mom and Dad chewing on anything of substance.

Principle #2: Teach Strong Character Qualities

Godly character is not promoted in our culture. A casual glance at the newspapers indicates that integrity, for example, is often a missing virtue among our leaders. Our culture values wealth. It values physical beauty. It values athletic prowess. But generally not character.

Since your child will not receive much reinforcement of strong character qualities *outside* the home, you are his only chance! What qualities would you like to see God develop in your young man or young lady? Several are listed in Figure 16.1 which you can study and discuss with your child.

These qualities will not only provide a rare and priceless foundation for your child, they will also make life a little easier for you. Take "wisdom" for example. Let's say your son has "embraced wisdom and she has set a garland of grace upon his

<table>
<tr><td colspan="3" align="center">**Developing Strong Character
Qualities in Your Child**</td></tr>
<tr>
<td align="center">**Contentment**
I Timothy 6:6</td>
<td align="center">**Gentleness**
Proverbs 15:1</td>
<td align="center">**Patience**
James 5:8</td>
</tr>
<tr>
<td align="center">**Courage**
Joshua 1:7</td>
<td align="center">**Helpfulness**
Isaiah 41:6</td>
<td align="center">**Persistence**
I Cor. 16:13</td>
</tr>
<tr>
<td align="center">**Courtesy**
I Peter 3:8</td>
<td align="center">**Honesty**
Ephesians 4:25</td>
<td align="center">**Self-Control**
I Cor. 9:25</td>
</tr>
<tr>
<td align="center">**Discernment**
Hebrews 5:14</td>
<td align="center">**Humility**
Proverbs 16:19</td>
<td align="center">**Tactfulness**
Eccl. 8:5</td>
</tr>
<tr>
<td align="center">**Fairness**
I Timothy 5:21</td>
<td align="center">**Kindness**
Ephesians 4:32</td>
<td align="center">**Thankfulness**
I Thess. 5:18</td>
</tr>
<tr>
<td align="center">**Friendliness**
Proverbs 18:24</td>
<td align="center">**Obedience**
Colossians 3:20</td>
<td align="center">**Thriftiness**
Luke 16:11</td>
</tr>
<tr>
<td align="center">**Generosity**
II Cor. 9:7</td>
<td align="center">**Orderliness**
I Cor. 14:40</td>
<td align="center">**Wisdom**
Proverbs 4:7-9</td>
</tr>
</table>

Figure 16.1

head." (Proverbs 4:8,9)[4] So you're in bed, it's 10:00 PM, and your son is out with his friends. Do you have cause to toss and turn, wondering what the car will look like, what he will look like, what tomorrow's front page will look like? Probably not. Because generally speaking, *wise people make wise decisions.* If on the other hand you have raised a foolish son, the converse is true, and he will likely bring "grief to his father and bitterness to the one who bore him." (Proverbs 17:25)[5]

Principle #3: Provide a Warm, Safe Environment

It has been said that the family is like a giant shock absorber for children. As a child grows up in today's world, his road will be full of pot-holes, and the only thing that will keep him from getting jarred silly is a family that loves him.

Sometimes I hear people say, "Don't *shelter* your children." Don't shelter them?! That's one reason families *exist*!

Imagine someone saying to you, "Don't enclose your child in a car seat. That will shelter him." You might say, "I suppose it will, but when he is young he needs some extra protection from an accident. Besides, even most adults have the good sense to wear a seat-belt, *because there are some things we should all be sheltered from.*"

The analogy holds when we look beyond the health of our children's bodies, and think about the health of their personalities. I believe young children need an extra dose of protection from ridicule, sharp tongues, biting sarcasm, and cruel comparisons (unlike the seat-belt example, these "accidents" are usually "on purpose.") And most adults have the good sense to protect their own personalities from attack—be it from chemical addiction, pornography, whatever. We still *shelter* ourselves.

Back to the home. This should be the place of all places that Johnny can run to, close the door behind him, lean against it, and breathe a heavy sigh of relief, knowing that he has come to a place of peace, of rest, of *sanctuary*. It's not happening. At least not in most homes. Parents bring home the stress of a thousand battles and they're neither prepared nor in the mood to give Johnny what he needs. One of the things Johnny needs badly is for his parents to *communicate with dignity*.

Ask yourself if you communicate with your children differently than you do with co-workers or friends at church. Here's a checklist we all can look at (or wince at) to see how we're doing:

> Do I interrupt my children?
> Do I snap at them?
> Am I sarcastic?
> Do I nag and "pick" at my children?
> Do I scream and holler at them?

You say, "Sure, but I do those things to everybody!" That doesn't get you off the hook. (It just means you're starting with the wrong book.) Most of us can do a better job of communicating with our children—and they'll be blessed if we do.

Principle #4: Build a Healthy Self-Image

The foundation for a healthy self-image (which doesn't lead to self-love or self-hate) rests on an understanding of God's character. On one hand, when I see His perfect character, I see my own utter unworthiness. On the other hand, by understanding the price He paid for me, I see my limitless value. It is in the balance of these two extremes that I can develop a proper, healthy self-image.

One practical way you can help nurture this healthy self-image in your child is by building what Dr. James Dobson has called *compensation skills*:

> Will your child collapse under the weight of inferiority, or will he use it to supercharge his initiative and drive? Will he "hide" or "seek"? The answer will probably depend on the availability of compensatory skills. And, I repeat, it is your job as a parent to help him find them. Perhaps he can establish his niche in music—many children do. Maybe he can develop his artistic talent or learn to write or cultivate mechanical skills or build airplanes or raise rabbits for fun and profit. Regardless of what the choice is, the key is to start him down that road early. There is nothing more risky than sending a teen-ager into the storms of adolescence with no skills, no unique knowledge, no means of compensating. When this occurs, his ego is stark naked. He cannot say, "I may not be the most popular student in school, but I am the best trumpet player in the band!"[6]

Another way you can build a healthy self-image is by giving praise—not for things your child cannot control, such as physical beauty—but for sincere effort. And do it without comparison.

Principle #5: Develop Self-Government

When Emily was first born, she didn't do anything for herself. Now I'm not complaining, mind you, but we had to do *everything* for her. Feed her. Wash her. Help her get around. Put her to sleep. Put clothes on her. Everything. Eighteen years of this and Carol and I are going to be wiped out!

But wait—they grow up, don't they? In fact Emily is already toddling around by herself, and she does something that looks a little like feeding herself. And her older sisters, Jennifer and Katie are doing everything I mentioned above, all by themselves—even going to sleep! (For a while, we called Jennifer the "taller-staller" and Katie the "smaller-staller." When Carol and I called for quiet from the living room, we became the "taller-staller-and-smaller-staller-callers.")

We all hope our little bundles of joy and helplessness will one day be able to take care of themselves. We originally made all the decisions for them, but they will eventually leave home and make their own decisions. (Although I did hear of some children asking their father how they could comfort him in his old age. "For starters," he replied, "you could move out.")

Then who will be governing that young man or lady? It won't be Mom and Dad anymore. Our prayer is that they will be *self-governing*—able to "rule" themselves under God's guidance. This progression is shown in the top chart of Figure 16.2.

But what if a child isn't young enough to be parent-governed and isn't mature enough to be self-governed? (We are only young once but we can be immature for a lifetime.)

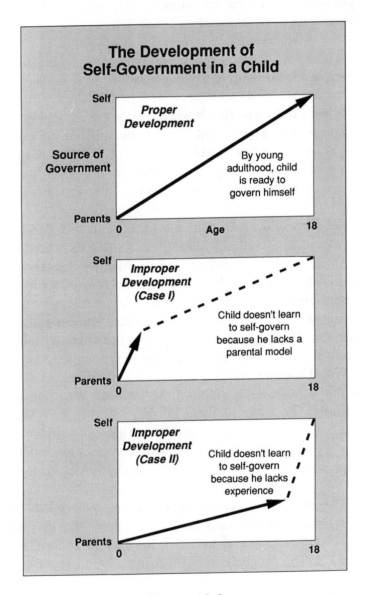

Figure 16.2

Who—or what—will govern that child? Let's look at two sad but common cases of improper development:

Case I: The child is brought into this world by parents who quickly pull away from their responsibility to guide him. Perhaps the most severe example of this is the street gang member. At an early age, this child is largely left to his peers. *Because he had no mature, adult model to follow, he never learns how to govern himself.* So who governs him? Perhaps his peer group...the detention home...the prison guard...

Case II: The child constantly hears the words, "Because I told you to." Expectations are set low for him, and his folks give him no opportunity to do things for himself, no chance to succeed, and no chance to make mistakes and learn from them. *Because he had no experience in governing himself, he doesn't know how to when he leaves home.* What governs him? Maybe his temper...alcohol...debt...pornography...

Ultimately, it is the child that suffers. How much better if the wisdom of Proverbs 16:32 could have been applied: "...(better is) he that ruleth his spirit than he that taketh a city."[7]

Principle #6: Practice Boundary Living

An excellent way to help your child become a self-governor, is to practice *boundary living.* Scriptural foundation for this is found in Luke 16:10: "Whoever can be trusted with very little can also be trusted with much..."[8]

Here is an example: When Jennifer and Katie were very young, we let them play in our fenced back yard by themselves. When they showed they could obey the rules there, we let them play in the front yard, as well. After they showed they

Principle of Boundary Living

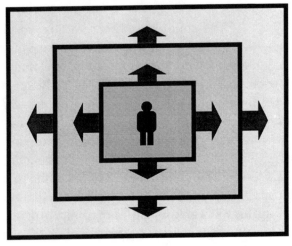

could follow the rules there (such as staying out of the street), we let them play with other friends on the block. Then, by their obedience, they showed they were ready to cross the street. This process will continue until, some day, I'll be handing each of them the car keys.

But we won't go from playing in the back yard to car keys all in one jump. The idea is to give the child a small "training ground" with clear, firm boundaries which are only extended *after* he shows he is capable of governing himself within those boundaries.[9] The child has the opportunity to fail on a small scale, when the consequences are small. This is important because *good judgment usually comes from experience... which usually comes from bad judgment.* The experience of earlier, smaller mistakes can bring wisdom to a critical decision.

Great, you say, but what if junior decides to cross over the boundary before you decide to move it? Ahh, that's the time for proper discipline (and not a bit sooner, as I'll explain.) I've heard that everything in the modern home is controlled by a switch except the children. That's a problem. In response to that problem, you can now read volumes about how to discipline with the rod: the shape of it...the best North American hardwoods to select...the recommended speed at impact...   But I also believe we're sometimes a little quick to "throw the book at 'em'" before we've shown them what's in the book. I think we'll find we need to use the rod less and have it help more if we follow these "three C's."

> *Clarify Boundaries and Consequences*—Set up firm boundaries ahead of time and make sure your child understands the consequences of stepping outside them. It's been wisely said: If a child doesn't know how to get a spanking, he doesn't know how to avoid one. Remember, setting boundaries is your responsibility; living within them is your child's responsibility.

Rules for Boundary Living

C larify **Boundaries and Consequences**

C onsistently Enforce Them

C almly Discipline

Consistently Enforce the Boundaries—If you find yourself saying "Son, I'm not going to say it again..." but you *do,* it's called inconsistency. So is coming home in a rotten mood and punishing your child for something that was OK for the last six nights. For your child, it's like playing football while someone moves the sidelines and end zones back and forth.

Calmly Discipline—If you've done the above two, you really don't have any choice but to discipline when called upon by your youngster. No need to get excited, though. In fact, Dobson has said, "anger assassinates authority." In his classic illustration, you are pulled over by a traffic policeman who, in a low, calm voice says, "May I see your driver's license?" You're a wreck as you fumble for it. Did he beat on your hood with clenched fists and scream in a shrill voice, "WHY DO YOU DRIVE SO FAST?!" Of course not. That would assassinate his authority. (For more on the subject of appropriate, loving discipline, please see Dr. Dobson's book, *Dare to Discipline*.[10])

If you have ever been in a home where these rules are not followed, you know it's not a pretty sight. A friend of mine, a pastor, was visiting a family with two boys who were regularly dipping into the candy jar on the coffee table to sustain their "buzz." The older boy wanted to get a book from the top of a bookcase, so he began climbing it, using the shelves like rungs of a ladder. In the process, many of the books came crashing down. The younger fellow grabbed my friend's suit pants with his candied hands, leaving a "clench-mark" for the dry-cleaners to remove. My friend said that debris covered the entire floor by the time he left in a somewhat shaken condition.

If your home is anything like this, I've got a message: Life is too short to live this way! You can do better. Research clearly shows that if families have 1) genuine parental love, 2) strict enforcement of boundaries, and 3) freedom within those boundaries, they will consistently produce successful, independent young adults with good self-esteem and enduring family ties.[11]

Principle #7: Learn Your Child's Love Language

In I Peter 4:8, we read, "Above all, love each other deeply, for love covers over a multitude of sins."[12] I don't know about you, but I'm always looking for anything that will cover over a multitude of my sins. This verse is for me. Now, what are some practical ways to love deeply?

Dr. Gary Chapman has put it in terms of five *love languages*. Everybody has one or two tried-and-true languages they use to show their love. And often they wait for others to love them back in the same language:

> *Acts of service*—Do you know someone who is always *doing* something for somebody? That's his or her way of saying "I love you."
>
> *Gifts*—Some folks have the love language of giving things. (My love language is receiving things!)
>
> *Words*—Others will express their feelings in words. The phrase "I love you" is not difficult for them to say.
>
> *Touch*—Physical affection is most important for some. Do you have a little guy who just loves to wrestle on the carpet? Maybe touch is his love language.
>
> *Undivided Attention*—I remember Jennifer sandwiching my head in her little hands and then aiming my squeezed face directly toward hers as she spoke. Now I'm a pretty observant kind of guy, so it wasn't too long before I figured out that she wanted more undivided attention from me.

If you and your child, or you and your spouse, have different love languages, it could be difficult to communicate love. If I only speak English and am trying to talk to someone who only speaks French, we've both got a problem. So find his or her language and begin speaking it. And practice using all five languages in your home. If you do, your multi-lingual children will be prepared to marry someone who speaks any language!

Principle #8: Enjoy Family Devotions

Howard Hendricks once said, "Whatever else you do, never *bore* someone with the Bible." Let's not waste that bit of sage advice on our families with episodes that begin with, "OK, kids, like it or not, you're gonna sit down and I'm gonna read the Bible now." Not when there are so many exciting ways to have family devotions. With a little effort, this can be a time that everyone looks forward to. How about trying some of these:

> *Biographies of Great Christians*—We've seen beautiful lessons written on the hearts of our girls as they heard how God worked in the lives of Susanna Wesley, John Bunyon, and others.
> *God-Hunt*—With the exciting material prepared by Chapel of the Air, *50 Days to Open My Home to Christ*,[13] your children will become more aware of God in their lives.
> *Bible Reading in Fun Settings*—Why not read the Bible early one morning in a cool spring meadow, or cuddle up by a fireplace with hot chocolate in a snowstorm?

Christian Tapes and Records—There are some fine Christian stories on tape and record that your children would probably love to sit and listen to. This can also be a good substitute for the Saturday cartoons.

"Flash-A-Cards"—A-Beka Book[14] has published a series of beautiful full-color Bible scene reproductions (normally used in classrooms); each set comes with a narration. Carol and I have found this to be a powerful way to remember selections from the Bible (and it's worked well for our girls, too!)

101 Hymn Stories[15]—In this book, Kenneth Osbeck provides some of the greatest hymns, and the stories behind them. At meal-time or bed-time your family can hear of the trials and triumphs of these saints of old.

Skits and plays—Last Christmas, Emily was just the right size to play Baby Jesus in our living room nativity play. (Guess who got to play the donkey!)

Songs of Faith—From my earliest days of childhood, I can remember cousins, aunts, and uncles gathering together in Grandma and Grandpa's little house tucked in the rolling hills of Pennsylvania. Grandpa sang bass, Grandma sang alto, and we'd all join in those old Gospel favorites like "On the Wings of a Dove." Ahh, what sweet memories.

Principle #9: Build Family Memories

Remember in the chapter on peers where I said parents need to be a fun alternative? We're here folks! Sometimes, I'm ready to "play" but my brain isn't, and no creative ideas come rushing forth. If you know this feeling, give Figure 16.3 a quick scan. If you don't see *anything* here that looks like fun,

I want you to sit down, and have someone put their index finger on your wrist...to check for a pulse. But first, let me entice you with a few of these.

It's summer time and you've got scraping and painting and fixing projects to last you a lifetime. But you look up in the sky, see the clouds moving briskly, and immediately sense a "higher calling." Before you know it, you and your family are all lying on top of a grassy knoll, your bare toes are wiggling in the grass, and you're watching your kite move lazily across the sky. Now, who needs to scrape that old paint today? And which memory will last longer?

Do you remember playing SPUD? Everybody gets a secret number. One person throws the ball up in the air, calls a number and everybody scatters—except for the person with that number, who grabs the ball, and yells "SPUD" to freeze everybody. The person with the ball then takes four giant steps toward the target of his choice (S-P-U-D), stops, and tries to hit him. (Not an altogether non-violent sport, I suppose.) When you get hit four times (S-P-U-D), you're out. The last time we did this, we had six adults and a dozen or so kids in the park playing—and did we get some strange looks.

How about domino tipping? One Saturday, we cleared a toy store of its dominos and took them home to play. For three hours, my girls, one of their friends, and I made the most impressive spirals, bridges, forks, and intersections to tip over. This dad was looking like quite the hero until the girls finally got tired and went out to play. Guess what I kept doing, especially since I had all those dominos "to myself"?

If you find something you *really* enjoy, your children usually pick up on the enthusiasm and enjoy it too. But that doesn't mean you shouldn't also ask them what they want to do. Friends of ours did this before one of their son's birthdays. His idea of a really fun birthday game was to have a *rotten tomato fight*. Since the family lived on a farm, this was not out

Figure 16.3

of the realm of possibility. They all made big piles of rotten tomatos, put on their rain coats, and went at it. Now, that's a family memory!

Chapter 17

Trends in American Education

"Awww, Ma. Do I *have* to go to school?" the son whined, "The kids make fun of me, the teachers hate me, and the superintendent is trying to get me transferred."

"I'm sorry, Son," she replied, "you're forty years old, you're the principal, and you have to go to school."

Well, maybe it's not *that* bad. But schooling in our country has changed over the last few centuries. In fact, if you are a public school graduate, you may be shocked when you see how much American schooling has changed in just one hundred years. Let's go back in time to America in the 1600's. If you were a Christian living then, there's a good chance you would have agreed with this thought by Martin Luther:

> I am much afraid that the schools will prove the very gates of hell, unless they diligently labor in explaining the Holy Scriptures, and engraving them in the hearts of youth. I advise no one to place his child where the Scriptures do not reign paramount. Every institution in which men are not unceasingly occupied with the Word of God must be corrupt.[1]

Does that statement grab you by the shoulders and shake you the way it did me? If so, I'd like to suggest that it's not because it is such a radical thought. Rather it is an indication of how far we have slipped from the original purpose of early American education.

In this chapter, we will examine three trends in American education that have taken place since the early 1600's: 1) home-control to state-control, 2) God-centered to man-centered, and 3) high literacy to high illiteracy. To do this, we will now travel chronologically down the American education timeline. If history wasn't one of your favorite subjects, please bear with me. These events of the past really are foundational to an understanding of the condition of education today—which we will examine in the next two chapters.

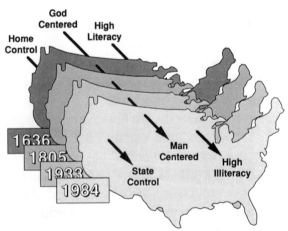

Three Trends in American Education

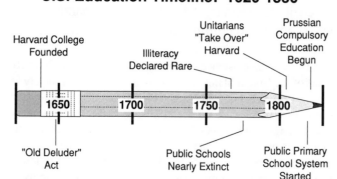

U.S. Education Timeline: 1620-1830

1636: Harvard College Founded—Harvard was established as a seminary for educating the commonwealth's future leaders. Feeder schools would be needed to supply this college with students.[2]

1647: "The Old Deluder" Act Passed—This Massachusetts law established a common school in every town of over fifty households. Attendance was on a purely voluntary basis, and the law was enacted to prevent that "old deluder Satan" from keeping men "from the knowledge of ye Scriptures."[3] So the reason we *have* schools today is to enable our children to read the Bible!

1765: Illiteracy Declared Rare—According to John Adams, foreigners passing through America and conversing with its citizens "have never seen so much knowledge and civility among the common people in any part of the world."[4] He reported:

> (A) native of America who cannot read or write is as rare an appearance...as a comet or an earthquake.[5]

1776: Public Schools Nearly Extinct—At the beginning of our nation, there was only one public school system (Boston), and even it left primary education in the hands of private dames' schools. According to Samuel Blumenfeld:

> Despite the existence of slavery in the South, the first fifty years of the United States was as close to a libertarian society as has ever existed. For education, it meant complete freedom and diversity. There were no accrediting agencies, no regulatory boards, no state textbook selection committees, no teacher certification requirements. Parents had the freedom to choose whatever kind of school or education they wanted for their children. Home tutoring was common and there were private schools of every sort and size: church schools, academies for college preparation, seminaries, dames' schools for primary education, charity schools for the poor, tutors, and common schools.[6]

1805: Unitarians Take Control of Harvard—With the expulsion of the Calvinists and their "narrow" view of a God-centered world, the Unitarians were free to promote their man-centered view: Man was not innately depraved, and education was needed to eliminate ignorance, poverty, social injustice, and crime.[7]

1818: Public Primary School System Started—In a complete reversal of forces in the free market, the Boston Unitarians promoted the establishment of the first public primary school system and the consequent phase-out of dames' schools.[8]

1819: Prussian Compulsory Education Begun—In Prussia, a state system of compulsory education, complete with truant officers, graded classes, and uniform curriculum, was established, which would later serve as a model for American education.[9]

U.S. Education Timeline: 1830-1880

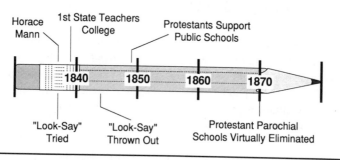

1837: Horace Mann Becomes 1st Massachusetts Board Secretary—With the support of the Unitarians, this crusader for state control immediately set himself to overcoming opposition to proposed state-controlled teachers' training.[10]

1837: "Look-Say" Reading Started in Boston Schools—The "look-say," or whole-word method, was invented in the 1830's by Thomas Gallaudet, as a method for teaching the deaf to read (who could not hear the sounds used in the traditional phonics approach.) Horace Mann heartily endorsed the new approach and it was immediately adopted.[11]

1839: 1st State Teachers College Established—Horace Mann and his followers succeeded in establishing the first such college—the Normal School at Lexington, Massachusets—and with it set the stage for greater state control of education.[12]

1844: "Look-Say" Thrown Out by Boston Schoolmasters—Common sense prevailed after a group of Boston schoolmasters leveled a blistering attack on Mann and his whole-word teaching method.[13]

1849: Protestants Support Public Schools—Initially many Christians were fearful of public schools; in 1840, Bishop Hughes clearly expressed his views:

> To make an infidel, what is it necessary to do? Cage him up in a room, give him a secular education from the age of five years to twenty-one, and I ask you what he will come out, if not an infidel?...They (public school proponents) say their education is not sectarianism; but it is; and of what kind? The sectarianism of infidelity in its every feature.[14]

Eventually, however, the Protestants decided the public schools needed the positive influence of their children. In 1849, the Protestant General Assembly of Massachusetts concluded:

> It is however a great evil to withdraw from the established system of common schools, the interest and influence of the religious part of the community...
> If after a full and faithful experiment, it should at last be seen that fidelity to the religious interests of our children forbids further patronage of the system, we can unite with the Evangelical Christians in the establishment of private schools, in which more full doctrinal religious instruction may be possible.[15]

This argument led to an "experiment" that was so "full and faithful" that more than a century passed before Protestant private schools were reborn!

1870: Protestant Parochial Schools Virtually Eliminated—Except for one Lutheran system in Missouri, the Protestant private schools had been wiped off the U.S. map.[16]

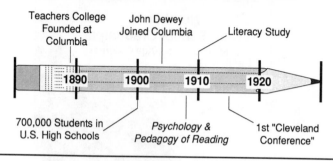

U.S. Education Timeline: 1880-1930

1889: Teachers College Founded at Columbia University— This is significant because its graduates generally didn't go off to teach 7th grade English somewhere; by and large they became the leaders in education—deans and professors at other teachers colleges, superintendents of school systems, etc.[17]

1900: 700,000 Students in U.S. High Schools—By the turn of the century, the American public education system was solidly established. Up from a total of only 69 public high schools in 1860, it was now ready to begin its real growth spurt in the first half of the 20th century.[18] (See Figure 17.1[19])

1904: John Dewey Joins Columbia Faculty—As the "Father of Progressive Education," Dewey exerted a tremendous influence over the course of U.S. education. Although an educator, he felt strongly that intelligence led to selfishness, which in turn led to that great evil, capitalism:

> The mere absorbing of facts and truths is so exclusively individual an affair that it tends very naturally to pass into selfishness...[20]
> The last stand of oligarchical and anti-social seclusion is the perpetuation of this purely individualistic notion of intelligence.[21]

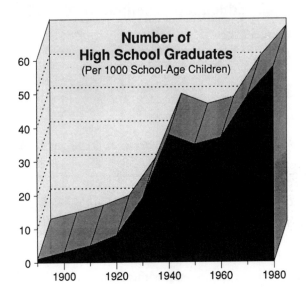

Figure 17.1[(19)]

Clearly, the next generation would have to be less intellectual and more social. Intellectual knowledge, in fact, was held in such low esteem by Dewey's teacher, G. Stanley Hall, that he wrote of the *virtues of illiteracy*!

> The knowledge which illiterates acquire is probably on the whole more personal, direct, environmental and probably a much larger portion of it practical. Moreover, they escape much eyestrain and mental excitement, and, other things being equal, are probably more active and less sedentary... Illiterates escape certain temptations, such as vacuous and vicious reading.[22]

1908: Psychology and Pedagogy of Reading Published— This book, written by one of Dewey's contemporaries, Edmund Burke Huey (a man who had never taught a child to read), was viewed as *the* authority on the teaching of reading. As such, it successfully paved the way for "look-say" by excusing word-substitution which would become common with this technique:[23] Huey wrote:

> Even if the child substitutes words of his own for some that are on the page, provided that those express the meaning, it is an encouraging sign that the reading has been real, and recognition of details will come as it is needed.[24]

1910: Literacy Study Completed—Even as late as 1910, our country's literacy rate was quite respectable, with only 2.2% illiteracy for children age 10 to 14. For many of the non-frontier states, the illiteracy rate was only 0.1%.[25]

1915: First "Cleveland Conference" Convened—With no minutes, no constitution, no officers, and no "public life," 19 leaders of the progressive movement began meeting together (with the first meeting in Cleveland). Their objective? Gradually, methodically change how and what American children were taught. Their tactics? 1) Exert influence over curriculum publishers, and 2) use "placement barons" in key administrative roles to insert loyal progressives into influential positions across the country. The "Cleveland Conference" progressives shared these views:

1) Absolute faith should be placed in science and evolutionary theory.
2) Children can be trained much like animals using the new behavioral psychology techniques.
3) Religion and traditional values are an obstacle to social progress.
4) Socialism is morally superior to capitalism.[26]

U.S. Education Timeline: 1930-Present

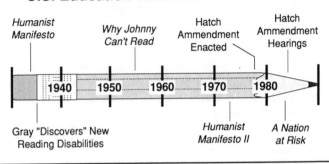

1933: Humanist Manifesto Written—John Dewey was a major force behind this document, which put forth the humanist position on a number of items, including religion:

> There is great danger of a final, and we believe fatal identification of the word religion with doctrines and methods which have lost their significance and which are powerless to solve the problem of human living in the Twentieth Century.
> ... While this age does owe a vast debt to traditional religions, it is none the less obvious that any religion that can hope to be a synthesizing and dynamic force for today must be shaped for the needs of this age.[27]

Imagine that. *Shape* a religion!

1935: Gray "Discovers" New Reading Disabilities—Dr. William Gray's "Dick and Jane" primers—the first attempt to introduce "look-say" since the early 1800's—were published in 1930. In five short years, students using them did so poorly that Gray felt compelled to blame the disaster on the students—not the teaching method. Blumenfeld reports:

> Gray...described a whole new syndrome of problems that were causing reading disability: mental deficiency or retarda-

tion, defective vision, auditory deficiencies, congenital word blindness, developmental alexia, congenital aphasia, dyslexia, congenital alexia, strephosymbolia, cerebral dominance, handedness, eyedness, ambidexterity, emotional instability, etc.[28]

1955: Why Johnny Can't Read Published—In this landmark book, Rudolph Flesch enraged the progressive education community by revealing eleven research studies that showed the phonics method to be superior to the "look-say" reading approach. The "look-say" technique required heavy repetition to memorize each word. Textbook publishing companies liked this because it required huge quantities of reading primers. But Flesch recognized that this dull repetition would quickly turn children off to reading. He wrote:

> The child is told what each word means and then they are mechanically, brutally hammered into his brain. Like this:
> "We will look," said Susan.
> "Yes, yes," said all the children.
> "We will look and find it."
> So all the boys and girls looked.
> They looked and looked for it.
> But they did not find it.[29]

According to Blumenfeld, "(Flesch) seemed to say: 'Look, you silly fools, phonics works better than look-say.' What Flesch didn't know is that the professors already knew that."[30]

1973: Humanist Manifesto II Published—The following excerpts from this document reveal the secular humanists' position in a number of areas:

> Religion: "...faith in the prayer-hearing God...is an unproved and outmoded faith."
> God: "No deity will save us; we must save ourselves."
> Ethics: "Ethics are autonomous and situational, needing no theological or ideological sanction."

Sex: "The right to birth control, abortion, and divorce should be recognized."

Government: "We affirm a set of common principles...(which) are designed for a secular society on a planetary scale."[31]

1978: Hatch Amendment Enacted—This amendment was designed to stop the extensive psychological probing and manipulation taking place at schools at the expense of scholastic education.[32] Earlier, the NEA (National Education Association) had made its position clear in one of its pamphlets:

> Schools will become clinics whose main purpose is to provide individualized psycho-social treatment for the student, and teachers must become psycho-social therapists. Children are to become the objects of experimentation.[33]

1983: A Nation at Risk Published—The National Commission on Excellence in Education issued its now-historic conclusion:

> ...the educational foundations of our society are presently being eroded by a rising tide of mediocrity that threatens our very future as a nation and as a people... If an unfriendly foreign power had attempted to impose on America the mediocre educational performance that exists today, we might well have viewed it as an act of war. As it stands, we have allowed this to happen to ourselves.[34]

1984: Hatch Amendment Hearings Held—In response to the general failure in enforcement of the Hatch Amendment, the U.S. Department of Education held public hearings in seven cities in March of 1984. The outcry was great as parents and concerned teachers supplied over 1300 pages of testimony. *Without exception*, the message was the same: children were being damaged by the "therapy" techniques employed in the classroom.[35]

Had you heard of the Hatch Amendment hearings? If not, you have lots of company. According to Phyllis Schlafly, there was no television coverage at all, and fewer than half a dozen newspaper articles in the entire country. If you did hear of the hearings, it was probably from her excellent book, *Child Abuse in the Classroom*,[36] in which half of the testimony is reproduced.

Home-control to state-control. High literacy to high illiteracy. God-centered to man-centered. This is the legacy of education in our country. Not very pleasant to look at, but essential to the understanding of *why* we are where we are today. And where exactly are we? In Chapter 18 we will answer that question in regard to the teaching of values; in Chapter 19, with respect to the teaching of academic knowledge.

Chapter 18

Value Lessons in the Public School

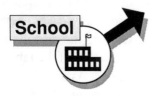

Many today are talking about secular humanism in the public schools. If I could do so in good conscience, I would avoid covering the material of this chapter entirely because, to put it bluntly, it is ugly.

My goal is not to "expose" the secular humanist with pointed finger and shrill voice. And I surely do not wish to heap guilt upon the Christian parent who by design or by default sends his child to public school. (It has been said that Jesus came to not only "comfort the afflicted," but to also "afflict the comfortable." In this case, many parents already feel "afflicted.")

The purpose of this chapter is simply to warn parents of *potential* danger so they are prepared to meet it. If a physician showed you a small tumor on your X-ray, you would want to get several questions answered without delay: "What is the nature of the intrusion—will it destroy my body if untreated, or is it benign? If treatment is recommended, what type— drugs, radiation, surgical removal? Should my body be fortified through diet or exercise to help ward off any threat?"

The best I can hope to do in this chapter is to show you the "X-ray." If your child is in a local public school, you can then determine if a dangerous disease is present there, the best method of treatment, and how you should fortify him at home.

Before I begin, I need to make two points. The first is that a vast number of public school teachers, many of them Christians, have nothing but the best intentions for your child. And, their values are, in many cases, very much like your values. For the most part, the problems come from the educational elite, the leadership of the labor union (NEA), the vested-interest publishers. And it is from these that our teachers receive their training, their textbooks, and their classroom materials.

The second point is that some school system superintendents have said, "That stuff's not coming in here." Don't assume that your school system has the problems covered in this chapter. But please, don't assume that there are no problems. (After my seminars, I've heard tales from too many parents in too many school systems to believe this is a safe assumption.) The only way to know...is to check.

The Agenda of the Secular Humanists

Just because a secular humanist wants something to happen in public schools doesn't mean it will. Yet, when we trace the intertwined history of American education and secular humanism since Dewey's work on the original *Humanist Manifesto*, we have cause for concern. And that concern can quickly turn to alarm when we hear the intent of the humanist:

> Something wonderful, free, unheralded, and of significance
> to all humanists is happening in the secondary schools. It is the
> adolescent literature movement. They may burn *Slaughterhouse*

Five in North Dakota and ban a number of innocuous books in Kanawah County, but thank God the crazies don't do all that much reading. If they did, they'd find that they have already been defeated. Adolescent literature has opened Pandora's box... Nothing that is part of contemporary life is taboo in the genre, and any valid piece of writing that helps to make the world more knowable to young people serves an important humanistic function.[1]

John J. Dumphy put forth the humanist position so well that his essay was awarded a prize (*The Humanist*, 1983):

> A viable alternative (to Christianity) must be sought. I am convinced that the battle for humankind's future must be waged and won in the public school classroom by teachers who correctly perceive their role as proselytizers of a new faith: A religion of humanity that recognizes and respects the spark of what theologians call divinity in every human being. These teachers must embody the same selfless dedication as the most rabid fundamentalist preachers, for they will be ministers of another sort, utilizing a classroom instead of a pulpit to carry humanist values into what they teach, regardless of the education level—pre-school, day care or large state university.
>
> The classroom must and will become an arena of conflict between the old and the new—the rotting corpse of Christianity, together with all its adjacent evils and misery, and the new faith of humanism, resplendent in its promise of a world in which the never-realized Christian ideal of "love thy neighbor" will finally be achieved.[2]

Imagine this scene: You and your allies are in a battle. Now the "other side" knows that it is in a battle, but your side doesn't! Are you at a disadvantage? This is exactly what has taken place for many years, and only recently have God's people become aware that they are in a battle for their children's minds.

Why did Dumphy write that the classroom must become the arena of conflict? Frankly, you and I are too old. It's too late to change us, but not too late for our children. It is an effective principle which was used, with a different objective, by Adolph Hitler:

> When an opponent declares "I will not come over to your side," I calmly say, your child belongs to us already... What are you? You will pass on. Your descendants, however, now stand in the new camp. In a short time they will know nothing else but this new community.[3]

Three years later, Hitler abolished all private schools. But what will humanists do? It may be hard to imagine them abolishing private schools. But will they use the public school classroom to undermine the values you have taught your child at home? In a message to 6000 California school board members, Dr. Ashley Montague announced:

> Every child in America comes to school "insane" at the age of six because of the American family structure.[4]

Why would he say that? Perhaps because, as a Gallup Poll revealed, 94% of Americans believe in God and 84% believe the Ten Commandments are valid today.[5] Another humanist, Dr. Pierce of Harvard University, saw the problem this way:

> Every child in America who enters school at the age of five is mentally ill, because he comes to school with allegiance toward our elected officials, toward our founding fathers, toward our institutions, toward the preservation of this form of government we have...the children are sick, because the truly well individual is one who has rejected all of those things and is what I would call the true international child of the future.[6]

Thus, patriotism is viewed as a sign of *mental illness*.

Strategy and Methods for Change

Secular humanists have adopted a strategy to eliminate the "insanity" and "mental illness" they find in young children. As explained by Dr. Joseph P. Bean, who closely examined the "new" social studies texts, the strategy is three-fold:

1) "Unfreeze" home-taught values and standards.
2) Give the child "different standards and a different concept of who he is."
3) "Refreeze" and "lock the child into the (new) self."[7]

Many methods have been used over the past three decades to carry out this strategy, a few of which are briefly described here:

Values Clarification—Over and over, the child is told there is no "right and wrong." He is encouraged to explore his feelings and is asked, "What is *your* value system?"

Moral Dilemmas—The child is given hypothetical, often bizarre, situations in which he has to choose one of several unpleasant or unethical options.

Role-Playing—Children are asked to role-play scenes which may involve anything from suicide to pregnancy.

Secret Diaries—The child is required to write a diary that includes thoughts on his parents, religion, sex, etc. In many cases, he is not allowed to take the diary home where his parents could read it.

Resistors Singled Out—In one example, a young boy was called on by the teacher 23 times in one class session to defend his position![8] His viewpoint had not been "refrozen" to agree with the instructor's.

Many of these methods came to light during the Hatch Amendment hearings mentioned earlier. (For a more com-

Aa Bb Cc Dd Ee Ff Gg Hh Ii Jj Kk Ll Mm Nn Oo Pp Qq

**Lessons Your Child Could Learn
in Public School**

1. You Should Question Your Parents' Values & Authority

2. Ethics Are Situational - Not Absolute

3. Christianity is Outmoded and Worthless

4. Your Allegiance Belongs to the World Community

5. Use of Alcohol and Drugs is Not "Wrong"

6. Sex is OK Outside a Heterosexual Marriage Relationship

7. It is Important to Study Death, Despair & Violence

plete description of the use of these methods, please see
Phyllis Schlafly's *Child Abuse in the Classroom* and Mel and
Norma Gabler's *What Are They Teaching Our Children?*)

As parents and concerned teachers have become more
aware of secular humanism in the classroom, a tidal wave of
examples has washed ashore. I have grouped these into seven
value lessons that children are being taught in many public
schools across the country.

Lesson #1: You Should Question Your Parents' Values and Authority

One third-grader was asked the following "unfreezing"
questions:

> Do you like your parents?... Would you rather live some
> place else?... Do your parents spank you?... Do you think that is
> child abuse?[9]

In other testimony before the U.S. Department of Education, the following classroom questions were revealed:

> What is the one thing your mom and dad do to you that is unfair?[10]
> How many of you ever wanted to beat up your parents?[11]
> Do your parents lie to you?... Do your parents hit you?... Why did they get married?[12]
> How many of you hate your parents?[13]

When the last question was asked at the beginning of a high school health class, only three children raised their hands. The teacher asked the same question at the end of the class, after the "lesson" was complete; this time all but three raised their hands.

According to further testimony:

> Parents in New Jersey tried in vain to stop Values Clarification from infiltrating their school. In doing a written assessment of the program, they could not find, they said, in any of the hypothetical situations, a single portrayal of parents in a positive manner. Parents were shown to be overreaching, nagging, unfair, overcritical of their children's friends.[14]

We could talk about the course called "Anti-Parent Pressure"[15] or the film called "Parents—Who Needs Them,"[16] but I think you get the idea. Not much time is spent on Ephesians 6:1, "Children, obey your parents in the Lord, for this is right."[17]

Lesson #2: Ethics Are Situational—Not Absolute

Imagine your child being asked to complete this sentence:

> The trouble with being honest is _____ [18]

Think of him answering this question:

> What would be the hardest thing for you to do: steal, cheat, or lie?[19]

Wouldn't you rather have him learn, "Ye shall not steal, neither deal falsely, neither lie one to another." (Leviticus 19:11)[20] There's not much that is "situational" about that, is there? And yet, the questions above are reaching our children in the public school classroom, while Biblical wisdom is excluded.

Lesson #3: Christianity Is Outmoded and Worthless

In "Three Cheers for Our Secular State," Paul Blanchard wrote:

> Our schools may not teach Johnny to read properly, but the fact that Johnny is in school until he is 16 tends to lead toward the elimination of religious superstition...[21]
>
> When I was one of the editors of *The Nation* in the twenties, I wrote an editorial explaining that golf and intelligence were the two primary reasons that men did not attend church. Perhaps today I would say golf and a high school diploma.[22]

It may seem hard to believe that the elimination of Christianity can be, for some, a higher priority than teaching how to read. Yet, as we recall the agenda of John Dewey and his contemporaries, we should not be surprised. This has led to such textbook passages as:

> A great many myths deal with the idea of rebirth. Jesus, Dionysus, Odin, and many other traditional figures are represented as having died, after which they were reborn, or arose from the dead.[23]

What would your child think if he read about the "myth" of Jesus' resurrection? In a textbook. Neatly typeset and "authoritative." Handed to him by his teacher.

Lesson #4: Your Allegiance Belongs to the World Community—Not the U.S.A.

Many fifth-grade students had this to learn about our country:

> No nation on earth is guilty of practices more shocking and bloody than is the United States at this very hour. Go where you may and search where you will. Roam through all the kingdoms of the Old World. Travel through South America. Search out every wrong. When you have found the last, compare your facts with the everyday practices of this nation. Then you will agree with me that, for revolting barbarity and shameless hypocrisy, the United States has no rival.[24]

Compare that to the following quote, which appeared in another textbook:

> (In China) marxism turns the people toward a future of unlimited promise, an escalator to the stars.[25]

But the textbook publishers are guilty of omission as well as deception. In a study of 45 history textbooks, how many times do you think this quote by Patrick Henry appeared? "Give me liberty or give me death." *Twice.*[26] Another fifth grade textbook devoted 7 pages to Marilyn Monroe, while mentioning George Washington only 8 times![27]

Why? Part of the agenda for secular humanists is to arrive at a one-world government. The NEA said in its *NEA Bicentennial Ideabook*:

We believe that teachers are the major resource through which to effect a world community based on the principle of peace and justice... We seek to make history rather than to recall it.[28]

Lesson #5: Use of Alcohol and Drugs Is Not "Wrong"

Here are some of the programs used in schools to teach children about alcohol:

Let's Get Acquainted With Alcohol[29]
Enjoy in Moderation[30]
How to Drink Responsibly[31]

Do you have the feeling that abstinence won't be heavily promoted? While these programs warn second and third graders of the dangers of excess, the children can be lulled into a false sense of security since they have been taught "how to drink responsibly."

And in spite of all the encouragement to "just say no" to drugs, we have had this type of teacher instruction:

Divide the class into five or six groups and let them spend about ten minutes on this question: "Should barbituates be used by someone as a recreational drug?"[32]

You'll notice the "answer" is given in the rest of the question:

"List the precautions that should be taken. What emotional condition should the user be in when using the drugs?"[33]

Lesson #6: Sex is OK Outside a Heterosexual Marriage Relationship

It doesn't seem all that long ago that I heard the rumble about sex education, and thought, "Sure, it's better if parents teach their children, but is it really *that* big a deal?" Then I started researching what was actually being taught and was shocked by what I saw! Common decency prevents me from repeating some of the material that our sons and daughters hear in co-ed classes, but I believe a brief history and some examples will give you a clear picture.

The Sex Information and Education Council of the United States (SIECUS) was formed in 1964 by Dr. Mary Calderone (later named "Humanist of the Year.") This organization was created to serve as a national clearinghouse for sex education material. Their position paper stated that, "free access to full and accurate information on all aspects of sexuality is a basic right of everyone, children as well as adults."[34]

A former SIECUS president described the problem as he saw it:

> Parents become traumatic about their youngsters engaging in sexual activity, because they do not realize that premarital sexual intercourse, even for children, is all right, provided consideration is given for the partner.[35]

Another SIECUS board member had a side business—publishing—which was described by Gary Allen:

> Rubin's pulpy Sexology magazine dwells on sex sensationalism, with lurid pictures of men and women in the most intimate positions, presenting crass articles dealing with the worst perversion. Examples of features in recent issues include: "Can Humans Breed with Animals?" and "Witchcraft and Sex—1968," and "The First Sadist," and "Wife Swapping in Naples,"

and "My Double Sex Life (the story of a bisexual)," and "Gangs that Hunt Down Queers," and "Why I Like Homosexual Men," and "Unusual Sex Demands," *ad nauseam*."[36]

With this foundation, it is not surprising to see the following passages in our children's textbooks on sex, homosexuality, and abortion:

> Sex outside of marriage is now socially acceptable... You determine your own value; what parents did may or may not work for you.[37]

> As evidenced by legislation prohibiting homosexual acts, American society frowns on homosexuals, *as it does on most things it doesn't understand* (Italics mine)[38]

> Abortion was accepted, and fairly common, in the United States and Europe until the early nineteenth century... Religious and ethical opposition did not develop until some time later. The situation has changed since World War II now that the danger of abortion to a woman is again less than the risk of a completed pregnancy, and abortion is, once again, legal in many countries.[39]

Some of the most objectionable material has turned up in teachers' instructions. Here are two examples which show how the normal inhibitions of children are broken down:

> Divide the class into small groups, segregated by sex this time. Ask the boys to draw the outline of a female figure (with felt markers on butcher paper) and the girls to draw the outline of a male. Give each group a list of the names of the parts of the reproductive system, males to girls and vice versa. And ask them to draw them in on their body pictures. Allow about five minutes. When finished, tape them to the wall. Ask the boys to correct the girls' drawings and the girls to correct the boys'.[40]

> Divide the class into groups of five or six. Select one word or phrase (of a sexual act or body part) and then have each group list as many synonyms as it can in three to five minutes... Now, rearrange the class in couples and ask that they engage in a conversation for three minutes, trying to use as many of the words on the list as possible.[41]

Let's think about this. These children are to come up with a list of words that you would be hard pressed to find grouped together anywhere else except on a restroom wall. When you were growing up, you might have had your mouth washed out with soap for saying *one* of them. Now, in some classrooms, teachers encourage children to use as many as they can pack into a short conversation.

But how widespread is the problem? That's not easy to say. We can get an idea by looking at one of today's biggest promoters of sex education—Planned Parenthood. According to George S. Grant (author of *Grand Illusions, The Legacy of Planned Parenthood*), Planned Parenthood is made up of more than 300 separately incorporated organizations, with 800 clinics, which directly affect 75% of this country's school districts.[42] This is an example of what they give us:

> The two women listened in dismay as the representative from Planned Parenthood reviewed her week-long session. She explicitly and graphically demonstrated in pictures and diagrams how to use various contraceptive devices; she used poor grammar and misspelled words as she gave out information that was medically incorrect—so obviously incorrect that even the teacher had to correct her at one point...
>
> The instructor discussed abortion and told the students that if they choose to have sex, and a pregnancy results, they then have another set of choices: they can either choose to keep the baby, which is difficult to do at their young age, or they can "get rid of it." Adoption was mentioned, but was discouraged as a viable option...

The woman told the children that free condoms are available at the Planned Parenthood clinic. She said, "there is a big basket of condoms just inside the front and back doors, and you can stop by anytime to pick some up." She apologized that the clinic was not closer to the school and said she hoped something could be done about that.[43]

Lesson #7: It is Important to Study Death, Despair and Violence

Do you remember the list of recommended read-aloud books mentioned earlier? One reason I get excited about those books is that I know our daughters are hearing some beautiful character-building lessons. But look what some "experts" would do. Textbook critics Mel and Norma Gabler report:

> Social psychologist Otto Klineberg compared fifteen American reading primers, including one called *Fun with Our Family*, and concluded that the characters—"gentle and understanding parents, doting grandparents, generous and cooperative neighbors, even warmhearted strangers"—were too *good*. He recommended that frustration, meanness, poverty, and crime be added for balance. Get this: He advised that educators study books used in the Soviet Union and Sweden to discover the levels of realism small children could handle.[44]

What a standard! Sweden has one of the highest child suicide rates in the world. How much better a standard would be, "whatever is true, whatever is noble, whatever is right, whatever is pure, whatever is lovely, whatever is admirable—if anything is excellent or praiseworthy—think about such things." (Philippians 4:8)[45]

Instead, our children are asked to think about these lessons of violence and death:

Tell a story. YOU are a murderer. WHOM do you murder? WHY? (You may think you are completely justified.) HOW do you do the terrible deed? Describe it in detail. How do you feel— as you work out your plans? as the victim's last moment approaches? at the instant of the slaying? afterwards? What happened?

TURNABOUT. YOU are the victim of a murder...[46]

For whom and what might you be willing to kill another person?[47]

Suppose you were to commit suicide; what methods would you most likely use?[48]

Children often have to do more than just verbally answer such questions in class. They role play their suicides.[49] They write tombstone inscriptions.[50] They practice writing suicide notes.[51] And what has this led to? The unthinkable. Children have been found dead—suicide victims—with their "home-work assignments" found in their pockets.[52]

Are Children Learning These Lessons?

It would not be fair or responsible to blame all of our society's woes on lessons learned in public school class-rooms. At the same time, we do see some fruit from each of the lessons learned (Figure 18.1).

While it's difficult to prove a "cause and effect" relation-ship in these cases, there is some strong circumstantial evi-dence. After three years of a "model" SIECUS sex education course in Anaheim, California, venereal disease was "out of control," and servicemen were found to be flocking to the area on weekends. When asked why, one marine gave a typical reply, "Man, everybody knows that the high school girls here are 'available.'"[53]

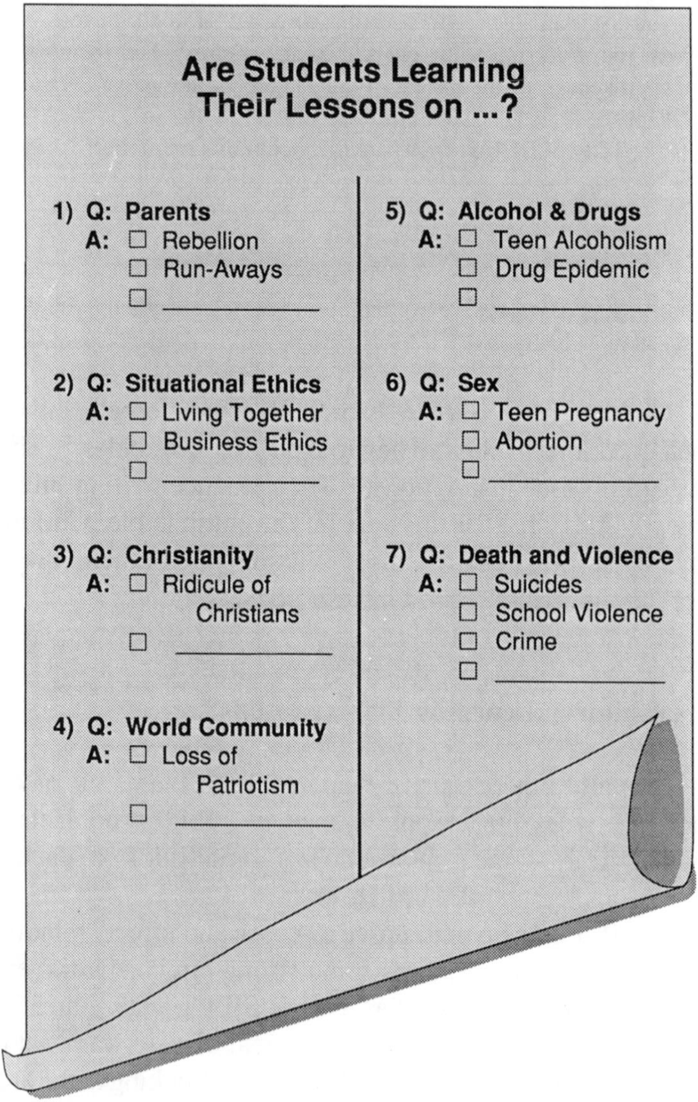

Are Students Learning
Their Lessons on ...?

1) Q: Parents
  A: ☐ Rebellion
      ☐ Run-Aways
      ☐ _____

2) Q: Situational Ethics
  A: ☐ Living Together
      ☐ Business Ethics
      ☐ _____

3) Q: Christianity
  A: ☐ Ridicule of
        Christians
      ☐ _____

4) Q: World Community
  A: ☐ Loss of
        Patriotism
      ☐ _____

5) Q: Alcohol & Drugs
  A: ☐ Teen Alcoholism
      ☐ Drug Epidemic
      ☐ _____

6) Q: Sex
  A: ☐ Teen Pregnancy
      ☐ Abortion
      ☐ _____

7) Q: Death and Violence
  A: ☐ Suicides
      ☐ School Violence
      ☐ Crime
      ☐ _____

Figure 18.1

The lessons on violence seem to have come home to roost right in the school hallways.   Each year, about 100,000 teachers are assaulted, with about 10,000 requiring medical attention.   A number of schools have installed the same type of metal detectors used in airports to find concealed weapons. The days are long gone when the "terrorist" in school was the principal with his paddle.

If you were a student in the 1940's, you may remember getting in trouble for offenses that would likely be ignored today.   Here's a comparison of top offenses in 1940 and 1980:[54]

1940	1980
1) Talking	1) Rape
2) Chewing gum	2) Robbery
3) Running in the halls	3) Assault
4) Wearing improper clothing	4) Personal theft
5) Making noise	5) Burglary
6) Not putting paper in waste-baskets	6) Drug abuse
7) Getting out of turn in line	7) Arson
	8) Bombings
	9) Alcohol abuse
	10) Carrying of weapons
	11) Absenteeism
	12) Vandalism
	13) Murder
	14) Extortion
	15) Gang warfare
	16) Pregnancies
	17) Abortions
	18) Suicide
	19) Venereal disease
	20) Lying and cheating

Do you see a difference in these two lists? For the most part, the 1980 list can be described by one word: felony! For many students, however, the true danger is not in the hallways; it is in their view of themselves. One young lady said:

> By Christmas of my senior year I sat down with my mother and started crying. I was severely depressed. I didn't know what I believed about myself. I didn't know who I was or anything. Even things I was positive about earlier, I just didn't know. I had to learn to know myself all over again. I had to learn what I believed all over again, using all the sources that the school taught me were outdated, such as my mom and dad, my pastor and my Bible. I had to learn to make decisions again, the hardest part of all, and one that now, four years later, I am still having problems with.[55]

I'm sorry if you feel like you've just been dragged through the mud. I normally like to shelter my mind from the unseemly, and as I finished slogging through piles of this material, I remember feeling physically ill. (Please remember, I was looking at cases from across the entire country; you won't find all these problems in all public schools.)

But now we're done. The next subject—while certainly not cheering—is to my way of thinking far less depressing. Next, we will discuss the quality of *academic* learning in public schools.

Chapter 19

Academic Lessons in the Public School

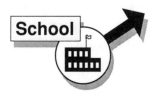

Columnist Dick Feagler voiced some common concerns about our nation's high-school graduates:

> "America has far too many people whose abilities aren't awakened." (Former Secretary of Education, T. H. Bell) That's true. Unfortunately America has far too many people whose abilities couldn't be awakened with dynamite. And an alarming number of them have been handed high school diplomas.
>
> Fifty percent of the kids who enter my old school never graduate. But let's forget about them for a minute and look at the ones who do. Many of them cannot read, write or add. Many of them cannot even speak. Sling these kids at any self-respecting college and they ricochet back like a bank shot in a billiard game. And end up assembling hamburgers at McDonalds—a corporation that has replaced the steel mill as the last refuge for the "unawakened."
>
> Furthermore, it is possible to spend four years in college without waking up, either. The spare bedrooms of thousands of American homes are stuffed with college-educated kids wondering just what it is they are supposed to do now.

> A friend of mine has a 28-year-old son who is still finding
> himself. So far, he isn't even warm. When he was let out of
> college, he went out to California for awhile to look for himself.
> Apparently he wasn't there. He returned home to his old
> bedroom and his old stereo. My friend was deeply depressed by
> this until he met a couple of hundred other parents in the same
> boat.[1]

You've just read an *opinion*. It's shared by many, but yet
remains an opinion. My question was, "What is the evidence?
Are children learning the academic lessons that parents send
them to public school to learn?"

Whenever you look at a complex question like this, there
is a danger of finding a simple answer—one that isn't accurate
because you've taken a bug's eye view instead of a bird's eye
view. Like the parable of the three blind men and the elephant,
you might see things differently depending on whether you've
grabbed the "trunk, tail, or leg." So I'd like to give you a
number of different perspectives. From ten different vantage
points we will now try to answer the question, "Are our
children learning their academic lessons?"

1. Standardized Test Scores

Perhaps the most publicized evidence of a scholastic slide
has been the SAT (Scholastic Aptitude Test) scores of recent
decades. This test is taken each year by over a million
students.[2] As shown in Figure 19.1,[3] scores are now much
lower than in the 1950's and early 1960's. The publisher,
Educational Testing Services, was concerned that the plummet was caused by test construction error or changes in the
test-taking population (such as more disadvantaged students
now taking the test.) They did a study and found a "scoring
drift," but it was in the *other* direction. When you look at
Figure 19.1, the recent years should be 8 points *lower*.[4]

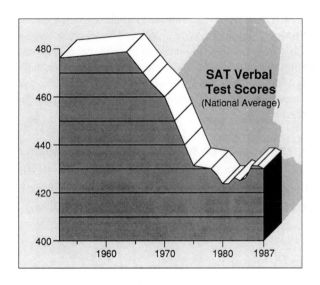

Figure 19.1[(3)]

The same trend can be seen in the SAT math test results.[5] It can also be seen in ACT (American College Testing) results.[6] In fact, according to the report of the National Commission on Excellence in Education, *A Nation at Risk*, "average achievement of high school students on most standardized tests is now lower than 26 years ago when Sputnik was launched."[7]

2. "Dumbed-Down" Textbooks

One of the most thorough researchers into the decline of learning in public schools has been Dr. Paul Copperman. He wrote:

> Over the past ten years, most of the major textbook publishers have instituted a conscious policy of rewriting their textbooks in order to reduce their readability to a level two years below the

grade for which they are intended. Thus eleventh-grade American history books are being rewritten to a ninth-grade level, and twelfth-grade American government texts are being rewritten to a tenth-grade level. This movement to reduce the readability levels of textbooks is widely known and accepted among secondary-school teachers and administrators, yet most parents have not been informed of it.[8]

Copperman goes on to say that these publishers can no longer sell a textbook unless its reading level is two years below the targeted grade level. Publishers who have bucked this trend have reportedly seen their sales dwindle.[9]

3. Grade Inflation

As shown in Figure 19.2,[10] schools began handing out higher grades much more freely in the 70's—at the same time standardized test results showed scholastic achievement was actually dropping.

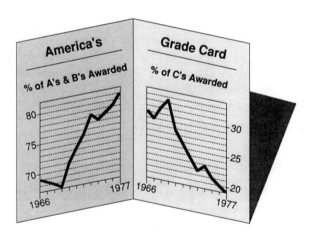

Figure 19.2[(10)]

Often this has led to a false sense of security by our youth. In an extreme (but not isolated) case, the *valedictorian* of a school was denied admission to college because his SAT math test results were in the bottom 5 percent and SAT verbal test results were in the bottom 13 percent.[11] After a repeat test (without time limit), the admissions dean said:

> My feeling is that a kid like this has been conned. He thinks he's a real scholar. His parents think he's a real scholar. He's been deluded into thinking he's gotten an education.[12]

4. Need for Corporate Retraining

In recent years, American companies have become alarmed at the lack of basic skills in their young employees. In fact, according to a 1988 survey, education has now become their #1 community relations concern.[13] Perhaps the most vocal captain of industry on this subject has been David Kearns, CEO of Xerox Corporation:

> American business will have to hire more than a million new service and production workers a year who can't read, write or count. Teaching them how, and absorbing the lost productivity while they are learning, will cost industry $25 billion a year, and nobody seems to know how long such remedial training will be necessary... It is a cost that I resent, because when business does remedial teaching we are doing the schools' product-recall work for them.[14]

5. College Remedial Courses

It's not just corporate America that is in the "re-work" business. The U.S. Department of Education reported that 82% of all colleges and universities offered some form of

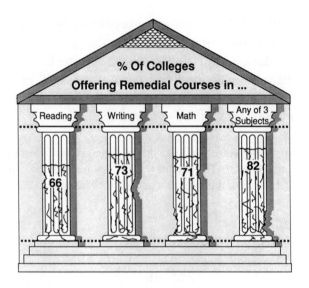

Figure 19.3[(15)]

remedial courses or programs designed to help students lacking basic skills (Figure 19.3[15]). Most of these institutions reported that enrollment in such courses was on the increase.[16]

6. NEA's Attack on Accountability

There has been a campaign, promoted largely by the National Education Association (NEA), to ban the use of standardized educational tests. Copperman wrote:

> If this movement is successful, American schoolchildren will no longer be tested with such tests as the Stanford Achievement Test, the Comprehensive Tests of Basic Skills, the Iowa Tests of Educational Development, or either the SAT or ACT.[17]

Why do I include this as an indication of a decline in academic performance in our schools? I believe it is the recognition (and attempt to hide), by some, of an educational failure. Copperman continued:

> The American public must not underestimate the desire of educators to avoid accountability. Until very recently, officials of both the NEA and the American Association of School Administrators were denying vehemently the existence of an achievement decline. If the evidence of the various standardized tests...had not been available, they would be denying it today.[18]

7. International Comparisons

Perhaps one of the most revealing perspectives on the academic achievement of our children is the international one. Clearly, American children no longer are among the world

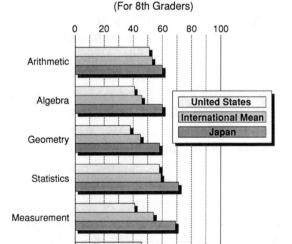

Figure 19.4[20]

leaders here. In nineteen separate international tests, American students were never first or second, and were *last* seven times compared to other industrialized countries.[19] Typical results are shown in Figure 19.4.[20]

This is particularly disturbing because many students haven't been told there is a problem. In describing a math test in which American students did poorly, Dick Feagler said:

> In that math test they gave, only 23 percent of the South Korean kids regarded themselves as "good in math." Yet they tested highest. Sixty-eight percent of American kids thought they were good in math. They tested dead last.
>
> It's bad enough that we're not teaching our kids. What's worse is that we're sheltering them from knowing how little they know.[21]

8. Functional Literacy Studies

The magnitude of the illiteracy problem in the U.S. has been carefully researched and documented in a number of studies. There are three areas of deficiency: 1) total illiteracy, 2) functional illiteracy, and 3) marginal literacy. If someone is totally illiterate, they are not able to read words. Functional illiterates are able to read many words, but are not generally able to link the words together to make sense out of them. For instance, such a person cannot read the directions on a can of soup, read a want ad, or address an envelope. The person with marginal literacy skills is barely able to perform these tasks.

According to the results of the Adult Performance Level (APL) study, 20% of the adult American population is either totally or functionally illiterate.[22] An *additional* 34% is marginally literate.[23] (Recall the high level of literacy in the study of 1910.)

9. Cultural Literacy Decline

"Do you have any hotels in New England?" asked the traveller. "I'm sorry, sir," replied the cheerful reservationist, "But we don't have any properties outside the United States."[24]

This true episode highlights a whole new type of literacy, *cultural literacy*, that is now being discussed as a result of the work by E. D. Hirsch. Culturally literate people share a body of general background knowledge, and can assume that this knowledge doesn't have to be explained in talking, teaching, or writing to each other. Hirsch gives an example:

> For instance, in my father's commodity business, the timing of sales and purchases was all-important, and he would sometimes write or say to his colleagues, "There is a tide," without further elaboration...
>
> For some of my younger readers who may not recognize the allusion, the passage from *Julius Caesar* is:
> > There is a tide in the affairs of men
> > Which taken at the flood leads on to fortune;
> > Omitted, all the voyage of their life
> > Is bound in shallows and in miseries.[25]

This was simply his father's way of saying, "Buy (or sell) now or you'll forever regret it!" It was short, it was forceful, and it was *understood*, because his colleagues were culturally literate.

Today, the U.S. Department of Education tells us,

> Most school teachers, college professors, journalists, and social commentators agree that the general background knowledge of American students is too low and getting lower. Surveys document great gaps in students' basic knowledge of geography, history, literature, politics, and democratic principles. Teaching is hindered if teachers cannot count on their students sharing a body of knowledge, references, and symbols.[26]

From a 1985 study by the National Assessment of Educational Progress, we learn that two-thirds of our 17-year-olds do not know that the Civil War occurred between 1850 and 1900.[27] Half cannot identify either Stalin or Churchill.[28]

If anything, the results are even worse in the field of geography:

- 95 percent of freshmen at a midwestern college could not locate Vietnam on a world map.
- Nearly half the students in a world geography class at a West Coast university could not find Japan.
- At "a pretty good university in Florida" 30 percent of the students could not locate the Pacific Ocean.[29]

Think of it! If you were blindfolded, I'll bet you could hit the Pacific Ocean on a map with at least 30% of your darts— it's a *big* ocean! Without a doubt, our children have been cheated. And Hirsch traces this problem to the desire by Dewey and his contemporaries to eliminate the "piling up of information."[30]

10. Comparison to Older Academic Standards

When our family first started reading the "children's books" written in the last century, I didn't feel terribly bright. It's not simply that the words were *different* because of changing dialect; it's that the prose was more *difficult* to read. Sentence length and structure, word complexity, and so on, all pointed to a higher reading level than I would have imagined for children. (Try picking up one of McGuffey's readers to get a good sense for this.)

I wondered, "Were children taught on a more advanced level than today?" You decide: Who do you think was asked to take the following test?

1) In what state and on what waters are the following: Chicago, Duluth, Cleveland, and Buffalo? State an important fact about each.
2) What causes the change from day to night, and from summer to winter?
3) What is meant by inflection? What parts of speech are inflected?
4) Write a model business letter of not more than 40 words.
5) A rope 500 feet long is stretched from the top of a tower and reaches the ground 300 feet from the base of the tower; how high is the tower?
6) Write a brief biography of *Evangeline*.
7) Give the structure of a muscle and the spinal cord.
8) Define arteries, veins, capillaries, and pulse.

These questions were asked of students in Indiana who wished to *enter* high school in 1911![31] Compare that to this question, which was asked of 17-year-olds in 1982:

Q: Estimate the product of 3.04 and 5.3:
A: _____ 1.6
        _____ 16
        _____ 160
        _____ 1600

How many do you think were able to handle the mathematics of "a little more than 3, times a little more than 5, should be a little more than 15"? 37% correctly estimated the answer to be 16![32] I realize we can't draw ironclad conclusions from a few test questions. Yet, taken together with the other perspectives, I believe we have to say that our children are not achieving their academic potential.

The point of all this is that we can do *much* better. Whether your child is in a public school, a Christian school, or a home school, there are things you can do to help your child soar far above the dismal and "rising tide of mediocrity" which we have just reviewed.

So if all my gloom and doom has left you slumped in your chair, please don't stop here! In Chapters 21-25 we will look at many fun, practical things you can do in *your* home. But first, let's carefully examine your three schooling options in the next chapter.

Chapter 20
Your Schooling Options

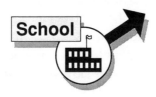

Public school. Christian School. Home School. These are the options from which the Christian parent must choose. I would like to say that I am now going to give you an unbiased view of each. But, if you have read the last three chapters, you know my opinion really cannot be described as unbiased. (For that matter, I have yet to run across a truly unbiased opinion on this highly charged and controversial subject.)

At the same time, I won't, and indeed can't say which option is the "right one" for your family. I don't know the age and maturity of your child, the strength of his spiritual convictions, the educational quality of your local public and Christian schools, your work schedule, your finances, the level of secular humanism in your public school system, and so forth. But *you* know these things. So let's look now at the three options so *you* can consider them.

Public Schooling

At one time, I was fully prepared to send our daughters to public school *by default*. What bothers me now is that I was

185

ready to do so without checking the schools out, without looking at other options, *without really thinking through* such an important decision. Oh, I had my reasons, but I hadn't challenged them:

1) "I went to public school and I turned out OK." When I hear this now, I respond with, "Did you?" I'm not trying to be unkind, but many of us set ourselves up as a standard without asking some tough questions: "Am I what God wants me to be today, or is what I learned (or didn't learn) in school holding me back? Or did it slow me down?" Obviously, I can't answer these questions for anyone else—but I do believe we need to think them through. An equally important question is, "Are schools different today than when I went?"

2) "Public schooling is the easiest for me." I never verbalized this one, but let's face it: What could be easier? After you get Johnny ready in the morning, this big yellow box comes rolling down the street and opens its doors. Poof! No more Johnny! It's quiet around the house. No muss. No fuss. No *cost* even. And then, much later, back comes the yellow box, the doors swing open, and out comes Johnny. Now, for some families, where both parents must work or single-parent families, this is a matter of necessity. For me, it was a matter of convenience with a little selfishness thrown in.

3) "I want my child to be 'salt and light' in the public school." Without knowing it, I was going to try to do something that had failed on a national level. (See the U.S. education timeline, beginning in 1849.) Let's see why this line of reasoning can cause problems:

> ...everyone who is fully trained will be like his teacher.
> Luke 6:40[1]

Thirteen years of training is what I would call full training. It's no problem if we have checked out the content of what is taught, and we're happy with it. But what if we're not?

> Do not be carried away with all kinds of strange teachings.
> Hebrews 13:9[2]

Have you heard of any teachings that were *stranger* than the seven value lessons discussed earlier? If your child is to go into a school in which these lessons are taught, the real question is: "Will my child be a *missionary* or a *mission field?*" If your child faces a humanist teacher or a humanist-trained teacher, we must ask who

...is in charge?
...is mentally developed?
...has been trained to persuade?
...can use peer pressure?
...has "supporting evidence" available?
(texts and classroom materials)

I believe children can best survive public school spiritually if the school has kept humanism out, or if the child is older and quite mature. (Too often we expect our 6-year-olds to be "salt and light" in a manner which Dad isn't even exhibiting at work.)

If your child is in, or will be going into public school, let me encourage you to do two things: *instill* and *examine*. From his earliest days, instill a reliance upon God and His Word so he *knows* what he believes. And examine what he'll be learning in school. No need to go in with your fist raised—go in with your hand outstretched. The truly concerned parent is so rare today that most teachers will be delighted to see you coming. If you are prepared and speak in love, you may help the teacher, the children, and many neighborhood families.

An excellent way to do this is by joining—or starting—a local chapter of CEE (Citizens for Excellence in Education). This organization, devoted to restoring "academic excellence, Godly morals, and traditional American values to the classroom," can provide invaluable resources. For more information, contact National Association of Christian Educators/ Citizens for Excellence:

> NACE/CEE
> Box 3200
> Costa Mesa, CA 92628
> (714) 546-5931

Christian Schooling

Christian schools began growing at a rapid rate in the last few decades (Figure 20.1).[3] For the most part, this growth has

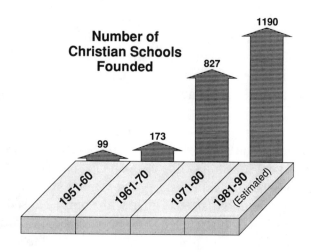

Figure 20.1[(3)]

been a response to the problems in public schooling which we've been reviewing. Christian parents wanted to know that their children would be taught Biblical values.

And what about the academic lessons? According to a 1983 study, students in ACSI (Association of Christian Schools International) schools scored significantly higher than students in public schools at all grade levels.[4] Eleventh-graders ranked about 16 months higher than the national average in terms of academic achievement.[5]

In a path-breaking study (in which he surveyed 58,728 students in 893 public and 122 private high schools), sociologist James Coleman shed some light on the reasons for this. As described in this review by Phil Keisling,

> Private schools are just more rigorous. Their students, for example, are more likely to have over an hour's worth of homework every night than are students in public schools. Private schools impose stricter disciplinary rules and maintain more order in their classrooms.
>
> Most important, private schools put a much greater emphasis on academic subjects. Seventy percent of their students are enrolled in an academic program compared with only 34 percent for public school...
>
> In other words, private schools demand more of their students—and they get more.[6]

Home Schooling

I remember when I first heard of home schooling. Carol had just visited a good friend, Karen, who had decided to home school. I had a lot of respect for Karen, but always thought she was just a *little* radical. So my first thought was, "Karen, what are you getting us into now?" My second thought was directed to her husband—and my close friend: "John, can't you do anything with her?"

It took about a year of watching home schoolers and researching the subject before I became genuinely enthusiastic. Now, in our fifth year of home schooling, I am completely convinced that this is the absolute best approach to education— *in the Adams' home*. If we talk about other homes, though, I lose my "expert status" and can only say that you would probably do well to at least look into it.

Most parents are familiar with public and Christian schooling. But since home schooling is a foreign concept to many, we'll go into a little extra detail here. What about academics?

- Dr. Raymond Moore, founder of the internationally recognized Hewitt-Moore Research Foundation studied thousands of home-schooled students and found that they have been performing, on average, in the 75-95 percentile range on Stanford and Iowa Achievement tests.[7]
- In Texas, home-schoolers scored a grade level above public-schoolers on average.[8]
- Home-schooled children attend many of the major universities including Princeton, Harvard, Brigham Young, and Yale.[9]

The most common concern about home schooling involves "socialization." Don't worry—we won't rehash the chapters on socialization and peer dependency. On a positive note, research shows children who start later in school tend to do better, not only in achievement and behavior, but also in sociability and leadership.[10] And in practice, all the home-schooled children I know are far from isolated—spending time with brothers and sisters, church friends, cousins, other home-schooled children, and neighborhood friends.

Beyond academics and socialization, there are often two remaining concerns: 1) Is it legal? and, 2) Am I qualified to teach? The laws and regulations vary greatly from state to

state, but in general there has been a strong trend to accommo-
date home-schoolers, largely due to their burgeoning numbers. For specific information about home-schooling legisla-
tion in your state, contact: Home School Legal Defense
Association, Paeonian Springs, Virginia 22129; (703) 882-
3838.

But can you do it? Think of the student-to-teacher ratio
you'll have, think of your ability to learn certain areas *with*
your child, think of the excellent curricula available for home-
schoolers, and think of the love and responsiveness you alone
will have for your own child. Also, 5 hours of classroom time
is equal to about 1-1/2 hours of tutoring time, so you needn't
spend more than 2-3 hours per day, especially in the first few
years.

Today, you can go to a number of places for help before
you get started:

1) Any of Dr. Raymond and Dorothy Moore's books
   will be very helpful; I especially recommend *Home
   Style Teaching*[11] and *Home-Spun Schools*.[12] These
   pioneers of today's home-schooling movement
   are well-respected for both their scholarly research and practical wisdom.
2) A subscription to *The Teaching Home* magazine
   (PO Box 20219, Portland OR 97220-0219) will
   "plug" you into the Christian home-schooling
   movement, giving you good suggestions and access to curricula and materials.
3) Gregg Harris offers *The Home Schooling Workshop*[13] which is extremely informative. Our family has benefited from Gregg's keen scriptural insights, many of which have found their way into
   these pages.
4) Become familiar with a local support group and
   your state organization; most offer conventions,

curricula exhibits, and moral support that you'll really appreciate.

I wouldn't advise you home-school because someone said you *should* do so. I believe it's best done by those who investigate and find themselves getting excited about the possibilities. Remember, it's not the only alternative...but it is one to consider.

If you're still wrestling with these options, I'd recommend you read *Schooling Choices*,[14] edited by H. Wayne House. In this book, three Christian authors, David Smith, Kenneth Gangel, and Gregg Harris put forth their most convincing arguments for public, Christian, and home schooling, respectively (and respond to each other's position.)

As you can see, there really aren't any easy answers. With public schooling, you need to address the value and academic lessons we discussed earlier. Christian schooling isn't easy on the budget, and you still have to keep a watchful eye out for peer dependency and even some "strange teachings" that can slip into textbooks. Home-schooling requires a time commitment, and you may find that some of your closest friends and family are critical of your approach.

Whichever road you travel, your child's success will be tied to *your* involvement. The greater the role you play—after school, on weekends, in the summertime, or during the schoolday—the more your child will benefit. In the next chapters we'll talk about specific strategies you can use to make learning "family-based."

Chapter 21
What is Family-Based Learning?

Let's travel back in time to the years before the founding of our country. Imagine you are a young girl growing up in one of the many rural homes in the colonies. You spend most of your time with Ma, learning by watching and doing. Together you gather food from the garden; some is prepared for tonight's supper, the rest is "put up" for winter. Your day is a busy one—long ago you were taught how to clean up around the house and how to keep an eye on your little brother. Tonight, after supper, Ma will help you with your reading or maybe part of the sampler you're having trouble stitching. She's even promised to let you do some of the sewing on your new Sunday dress!

If you are a young boy, you see a lot of Pa. Your day starts early as you both milk the cows and feed the animals. This morning you watch as one of the pigs is slaughtered; then Pa begins to tell you how you can help him smoke the meat later. You've already been shown how to use most of his tools, so you get the job of fixing the gate. There's no work in the field today—spring planting is a distant memory, and harvest is still weeks away. So you help Pa make more bullets. He said he'd take you hunting with him tomorrow! After supper, he lets you take a few "licks" on his fiddle and you're starting to feel grown up.

But time marched on. Our country was changing and technology was advancing. For understandable reasons, our children began spending more of their time in the school-house. Not too much, though. As recently as the early 1800's, Abe Lincoln spent only one year of his life attending school while growing up. Instead, he read, he worked, he traveled the Mississippi, he *learned* from *life*.

So now where are we? Today, we rely upon institutions—not the home—for teaching our children practically everything. Ask yourself these questions:

Where Will My Child Learn. . .

How to use tools ⟶ **Shop Class?**
How to swim ⟶ **YMCA?**
How to read ⟶ **Grade School?**
Bible verses ⟶ **Sunday School?**
How to cook ⟶ **Home Economics?**
To draw or paint ⟶ **Art Class?**
About our heritage ⟶ **History Class?**
About his body ⟶ **Health Class?**
To play an instrument ⟶ **Band?**
God's physical laws ⟶ **Science Class?**
To appreciate nature ⟶ **Boy Scouts?**
To do physical exercise ⟶ **Gym Class?**

? ? ? ⟶ **Home?**

What do most American moms and dads teach their children today? We are told to diligently teach our children (Deuteronomy 6:6-7), to train them up in the way they are to go (Proverbs 22:6).

Is all institutional learning wrong then? I surely don't think so. But I do believe that the pendulum has swung much too far away from the home and toward the institution as the center of learning. Parents don't need a certificate to teach their children—they need time and perhaps a little more confidence.

In the next four chapters we will talk about ways in which you can begin swinging the pendulum back to your home. We'll talk about *family-based learning.* This is a term we'll use to describe any learning that takes place under the guidance of parents. Specifically, we'll look at four types of family-based learning:

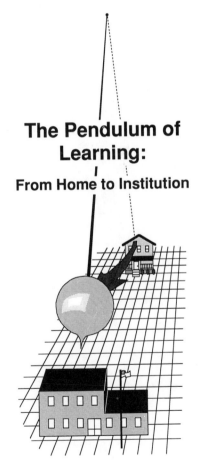

The Pendulum of Learning:
From Home to Institution

1. Creative Play—suggestions to help you develop creativity in your young child.

2. Work Education—practical steps to instill a good work ethic and teach useful work skills.

3. Family Learning Activities—fun activities for the whole family designed to give your child a love for learning.

4. *Home Tutoring and Schooling*—the benefits of either supplementing your child's classroom work after school, or starting your own home school.

Chapter 22
Creative Play

Family-Based Learning

A mother held the toy in her hand, slowly turning it over as she examined it. "Isn't this a little complicated for a small child?" she asked the clerk.

"It's an educational toy, Ma'am," he replied, "...designed to adjust the child to the world we live in. Anyway he puts it together—it's *wrong*."

Now, that's no way to let a child play, is it? But what is the best way? What toys should you buy? Should you play with your child, or will that "stifle" him? These are important questions, because so much of a child's personality is developed in the pre-school years.

Some Suggestions

1) Allow time for play: There is a danger of not allowing our children enough time to play. Between the time pressures of gymnastics, piano lessons, swimming lessons, and homework, we can fill up their little lives until they are as harried as we are! Think back to when you were young. Did you seem to have hours on end to play make-believe and let your imagination run wild? Check your child's schedule to make sure he has the same opportunity. English educator and author Charlotte Mason once wrote:

> ...organised games are not *play* in the sense we have in view. Boys and girls must have time to invent episodes, carry on adventures, live heroic lives, lay sieges and carry forts, even if the fortress be an old armchair; and in these affairs the elders must neither meddle nor make.[1]

Try to minimize the amount of time your child spends in structured activities such as organized sports, pre-school, video games, television, etc. These are time-gobblers that don't allow him to fully use his imagination and build his creativity. He needs unstructured time that will let his mind wander so he can be anybody, and do anything, and be anywhere.

2) Play with your child: I'm not saying you should be with your child all the time he is playing. But do take some time to get down on the carpet and enter his world. By giving a toy some of your attention, by showing him some new ideas, by responding to his efforts, you will be a *sparkplug* that ignites his creativity. In fact, research shows that parental involvement during play time is one of the two strongest contributors to learning development in small children.[2]

3) Provide Materials: In the research mentioned above, this was the second critical factor for stimulating mental development.[3] But what kinds of things to play with? Most researchers recommend you provide simple toys and materials that allow the child to use his creativity—not the toy manufacturer's creativity. It often seems that the less money the toy company charges, the better the toy. For this reason,

I'm not too enthused about animals and dolls that can sing, tap dance, and calculate the square of the hypotenus while reading the children a bed-time story. Depending on the age of your child, you might try:

> cardboard boxes to climb into
> building blocks
> old clothing for dress-up
> plastic bottles that can be filled up
> large sheets of wrapping paper
> paint and brushes
> modeling clay
> paper and scissors
> blankets and chairs for a tent
> xylophone
> balls of various sizes and materials

Paper, clay, paint. Isn't this a Madison Avenue executive's nightmare? One other word: Limit your child's time with coloring books. Some experts believe that overexposure to "keeping within the lines" can undermine creativity in a child.[4]

4) Ensure a "creatively safe" environment: It is important that your child knows he can experiment freely without being ridiculed or criticized. (Unless of course his "experiment" involves permanent markers and your wallpaper.) You don't have to "oooh and ahhhh" every creation, but you can ask him questions about that new "abstract" drawing, be complimentary of a new masterpiece, make a refrigerator door art gallery, and exercise wisdom in suggesting improvements.

5) Encourage outdoor play and free exploration: Decades ago, outdoor fun was a large part of nearly everyone's childhood. Whether at a farm or a city park, it is important that your child also have this time. Susan Schaeffer Macaulay asked:

> Do the children know the feel of dew-fresh grass on their bare feet, and lush freshness of the shade of a leafy tree on a hot afternoon? Do they know the fun of autumn leaves, and the fairy-tale beauty of an icy morning? Wherever the child lives in the world, we should consider his contact with nature as part of his life.[5]

The Playing Environment

Several studies have been made to determine how the physical environment for playing affects a child's mental development. As shown in Figure 22.1,[6] three factors—good

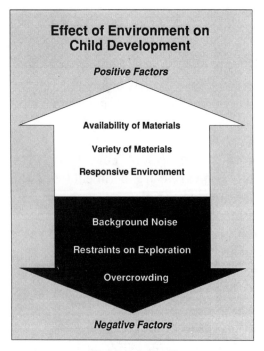

Figure 22.1[6]

availability of play materials, a variety of materials, and a responsive environment—positively affect the child's development. On the other hand, three other factors—high background noise, physical restraints on exploration, and overcrowding—are negative forces on this development.

Think about those negative factors for a moment—background noise, physical restraint on exploration, and overcrowding. Couldn't these describe many daycare centers? This is another reason to have your child in something close to a home environment if you must leave him.

As much as you are able, then, let your child explore. Let him have lots of different things to play with. And let him have fun!

Chapter 23

Work Education

Family-Based Learning

"Opportunity is missed by most people because it is dressed in overalls and looks like work." These words ring all the truer because they were spoken by that ultimate hard-worker, Thomas Edison. While Edison was laboring over one of his many inventions, a young reporter asked him how he felt about failing 10,000 times. He replied, "Young man, since you are just getting started in life, I will give you a thought that should benefit you in the future. I have not failed anything 10,000 times. I *have* successfully found 10,000 ways that will not work."[1]

Look at the backgrounds of most leaders today and you'll see hard work etched all over them. Several years ago, Warner and Swasey ran this ad:

Order of the White Jacket. At the annual Homecoming of William and Mary College in Virginia, you might see a famous governor, or a college president, or any number of prominent business and professional people, proudly wearing a white jacket. The jackets signify that these men earned all or most of their way through college, waiting on tables.

> They weren't ashamed of menial labor, they didn't hold out for the job they liked, they didn't ask for government help—*they waited on tables*, and it helped them earn the education they have since put to such splendid use.
>
> The order of the White Jacket has a roster of which any group in the land could well be proud. Perhaps there ought to be a chapter on every college campus in America.[2]

In these days of affluence, however, many children grow up thinking work is something to avoid. Ask somebody running his own business if there is any truth to the saying, "It's hard to get good help these days." Or go to a college campus and see how seriously some of the young men are working at their education—paid for by their parents.

The child reared to appreciate the blessings of a job well done has a tremendous advantage. With confidence in his ability to produce, spring in his step, and eagerness in his voice, what employer or customer won't want to be associated with him? And *you* can pass this gift along to your child. The key is to start good work habits early, for habits are to life as railroad tracks are to a train. Day by day, mile by mile, they take us toward our destination.

The Benefits of Work Education

The first—and I believe most important—benefit of learning to work at home is in developing the right *attitude*. Lamentations 3:27 tells us, "It is good for a man to bear the yoke while he is young."[3] Why when he is young? Because this is the best time to learn qualities that will serve as a foundation for an entire lifetime of work:

> Perseverance
> Responsibility
> Cooperation

Creativity
Deferred Gratification
Punctuality

The list could go on and on. Also, as part of his "training ground," this is the *safest* place to learn the lessons of business. Someone once defined business as the occasion when a man with money meets a man with experience. The man with the experience gets the money, and the man with the money gets the experience. The sooner your child has wisdom in handling his financial matters, the better. As many have learned, this wisdom doesn't come from age—it comes from experience.

The second benefit of work education is in gaining work skills. "Do you see a man skilled in his work? He will serve before kings; he will not serve before obscure men." (Proverbs 22:29)[4] Your child can learn many skills that will directly or indirectly prepare him for employment—or even his own business. A few examples are:

Budgeting
Phone Etiquette
Making Change
Salesmanship
Use of Tools
Handling Complaints
Interpersonal Skills
Computer Experience

Examples of Work Education

Family Chores—Long before school-age, you can have your little one begin to help you around the house. Would it be easier to just do it yourself at first? You bet. But remember, work is part of his education. The story is told of a farmer who worked his boys hard on the farm. When a neighbor pointed out that he didn't need to work them that hard to raise a crop, he quietly replied, "I'm not just raising crops, I'm raising boys."

Our girls have helped us with many little chores around the house, sometimes struggling, but still putting everything they had into it. One day, while watching one of them, I just had to help a little. I said, "Here, Honey, let Daddy help you nail in the next piece of aluminum siding." Well, maybe that wasn't one of their chores—but here are some examples from our home and others':

Dusting	Feeding Pets
Cleaning Fishtank	Emptying Trash
Washing Dishes	Watering Plants
Setting Table	Polishing Furniture
Vacuuming Carpet	Raking Leaves
Sweeping	Making Beds
Washing Windows	Trimming Lawn

It is important to start your child off on the right foot: 1) Cheerfully work alongside him when possible so he doesn't feel as though he's been sent off to work the salt mines alone. You might even...well...*whistle* while you work. Demonstrate the idea that work and drudgery are not synonyms. 2) If you see that he is in over his head, make the job simpler or save it for later. 3) To build that consistent "railroad track" habit, it helps to start with a weekly chart to check off. Then reward him for consistency. 4) Most importantly, heap praise on him for a job well done. More than anything else, this will help a child *enjoy* work.

Out-of-the-Home Jobs—As your child enters the teen years, there are many ways for him to earn money. Paper routes, baby-sitting, and lawn-mowing are some fine, traditional approaches. As his parent, though, your primary aim isn't to see that his wallet is full—but rather that his mind is full. Are there some creative ways you can help your youngster "earn and learn"? Gregg Harris tells the story of a high-schooler who was ready to mow lawns for the summer, but his dad had a better idea. That young man dressed up in a business suit, borrowed his dad's briefcase, and visited local businesses, offering a "satisfaction-guaranteed" lawn care plan. With the agreements in hand, he then distributed the work to his friends. He *earned* a lot of money, but more importantly, he *learned* valuable supervising, sales, and accounting skills. Here are some more ideas:

1) Establish a garage sale service. Many folks have things they want to get rid of, but not enough to bother with a garage sale. By holding regularly-scheduled, well-organized garage sales, your youngster could sell these items for them and collect a percentage. A good first step would be to produce a flyer that gives garage sale dates, rates, suggestions on condition of items, and drop-off and pick-up times.

2) Does your child have a particular skill or talent? By teaching computer skills, giving musical instrument lessons, or tutoring an academic subject, he'll be learning how to teach others as he earns money. As the saying goes, "He who teaches learns twice."

3) If your child is computer-literate, there are many software programs that could be used in a small business venture. Ideas include making personalized greeting cards, producing mailing labels, word processing, designing and publishing newsletters for or-

ganizations, typesetting resumes, and printing a neighborhood directory. Some children have even established thriving computer "bulletin boards."

4) Make a list with your child of jobs that most people dislike. The more the job is avoided the better. Perhaps your youngster can start a business cleaning garages, cleaning fishtanks, painting house numbers on curbs, or resurfacing driveways. After he learns the ropes, he may want to focus on the promotion and management side and get help from dependable friends.

Cottage Industries—This is where the whole family works together on a venture. It could be duplicating audio cassette tapes, building picture frames, making candles, or silkscreening T-shirts or Christmas cards. You might go to the library together and review books for ideas, and then "brainstorm" together as a family. The blessing of the cottage industry is that the whole family can share the rewards of its labor—by taking a special vacation, buying some family toys and games, or even allowing Mom to stay home.

For some time, I've been thinking of a "reward" I'd like to have for our family. We publish and sell sets of cards containing family learning activities. The girls help by testing the activities out, collating the cards, and answering questions at an occasional vendor's table. At the rate we're earning money, we'll be able to take our girls on a vacation to Europe... about the time they're in their mid-30's! But let me share my dream: We could pull out maps and study the geography of the countries we'd visit. And work a little. Learn about the history of those countries. And work a little. Study gothic and baroque architecture, learn some foreign language, try European cooking, become acquainted with foreign currency, read about the great European authors, politicians, and playwrights. And work a little more. Now, I ask you, would we have to drag our children by their wrists into St. Paul's Cathedral? Would they be looking for a Big Mac when we strolled down the Champs Elysées of Paris? Would they be bored during a Shakespeare play at Stratford-On-Avon? I believe they would get a lot out of the trip because they put a lot into it.

Family chores, out-of-home jobs, and cottage industries. All ways to rear a young adult who's not afraid to roll up his sleeves and tackle some work. Not afraid? He'll probably *enjoy* it. Ultimately, the highest reward for our work is not what we get *for* it, but what we become *by* it.

Chapter 24

Family Activity Learning

Family-Based Learning

Imagine this scene. Mom is trying to tutor Jimmy in one of his subjects. She hands him his workbook and says, "Honey, go to the table and work on pages 14-17." It's the same thing the next day and the day after that. After awhile, Jimmy thinks, "You know, Mom never comes with me. She'd rather do the dishes and I *know* she doesn't like that. This learning business must not be much fun."

Now let's try it again; we'll make Dad the hero this time. He comes home and says, "Hey Jimmy; after supper, betcha I can crush this empty tin can without touching it! Wanna see?" Jimmy thinks, "Sure, I'll stick around for *that*."

Later, Dad pours a half-inch of water into the can, and brings it to a boil on the stove (with the cap off). Then he turns the heat off, and plugs the opening with a rubber stopper. As the can slowly crumbles—as if by a giant invisible hand— Dad explains: At first, the tremendous weight of air (nearly 15 pounds per square inch) *outside* the can was offset by the steam *inside* the can. When the steam cooled and condensed, there was nothing left to resist the outside pressure. That's called a vacuum.

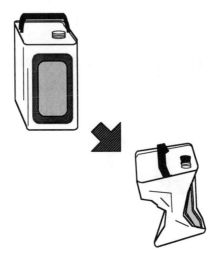

Jimmy looks at his dad's face and sees excitement. He looks at his mom and sees she's enjoying herself. She's cleaning up Dad's mess—but still having fun. And Jimmy says to himself, "I think I like this learning stuff."

And that is precisely the goal of family activity learning—to teach your child that learning is fun and to give him a *love for learning*. For the most part, you use non-seatwork activities. Your family will be exploring and discovering with all five senses—vision, hearing, touch, taste, and smell. And you can do it to meet *your* family's schedule, after school, on weekends, during summer vacations, or as part of a home school.

The Need for *Thinking* in America

Is this type of learning time-intensive for parents? Definitely. But is it needed? Absolutely. It helps a child to grow into an adult who really thinks—an uncommon occurrence. George Bernard Shaw once explained:

> Few people think more than two or three times a year. I've
> made an international reputation for myself by thinking once or
> twice a week.[1]

That may be an overstatement, but we generally don't do too much active, critical thinking. Instead, we tend to go through our routines each day on autopilot: Get ready in a morning fog, listen to the radio on the way to work, do the chicken-with-its-head-cut-off routine at work, drive back home (more radio to replace thinking), collapse in a chair with the paper, eat supper, become "couch potatoes" with the TV on, stumble off to bed, and then start all over. Much of the thinking we do experience is what Dr. Karl Albrecht terms "mechanical thinking."[2]

A mechanical thinker has a low level of curiosity and a general fear of ambiguity. The words "I don't know" scare him to death and will never be heard leaving his lips. He relies on "pat answers" and blindly reacts to buzz words. For this reason, it is relatively easy for advertisers and politicians to predict and manipulate his decisions. And he or she seldom reads, except for the sports page and the check-out counter "National Slanderer" magazines. In short, the mechanical thinker does not enjoy learning. He has taken the vaccination approach to education: "More learning? No thank you, I've already got my diploma."

With activity learning, you teach your child that learning is fun, and they won't *want* to stop when they are 18 or 22 (or 75 for that matter). It allows them to retain the creativity that God gave them when they entered this world. Researchers studied 45 year-olds and found that only 2-3% were "highly creative."[3] They then tested younger subjects; the results are shown in Figure 24.1. There seems to be a great loss in creativity at about the time children enter school. It has been said that many teachers prefer children of high intelligence and low creativity. Why? Because the learning process for a

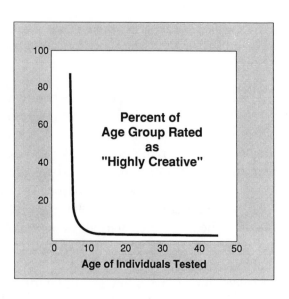

Figure 24.1[(3)]

highly creative child looks much like "goofing off." If I had
a roomful of 25 kids, *I'd* probably want them to be low in
creativity too!

Benefits of Family Activity Learning

In addition to helping your child retain the creativity and
love for learning he was born with, there are other benefits of
family activity learning:

1) Fosters Deeper Understanding—Years ago, someone
explained to me why I should study the Bible for myself.
"Discovery is the key to conviction," he said. And today, I
remember the scriptural insights I've "discovered" better than
those I've heard in a sermon. In like manner, your child will
gain a much better understanding of gravity, map-making, or
color mixing if he "discovers" them, than if he hears about

them in a classroom or reads of them in a textbook.

2)Develops "Real-Life" Problem-Solving Skills—Agatha Christie once said that classroom problems are "too arranged." This innovative, home-taught author knew that children need more than textbooks and workbooks and homework assignments to apply those principles they are learning. They need real-life problems to solve.

3) Allows Teaching of "Non-Classroom Subjects"— Imagine teaching your child how to be a competent public speaker, or passing along to him certain memory techniques to remember long shopping lists or people's names. These skills are not typically taught in a classroom, but can be taught and practiced in the home. In fact, they are probably best taught on a one-to-one, master-to-student basis.

4) Gives Close-Knit Family Time—Parents are sometimes stumped as to how to fill the vacuum they create when they limit TV and peer time for their kids. Family activity learning is a great "excuse" to gather the troops together. Whether around the kitchen table, in the shop, or at a nearby park, you can share "what if" questions, some laughs, and a good time.

Examples of Family Learning Activities

So let's look at some examples. Here are some favorites that bring big silly grins to my face. You can do them without much preparation, you don't need to sink a lot of time into them, and they're fun. In fact, you may want to put this book down in a few moments and try one!

1. The Air Rocket: Here's how you and your child can build an "air rocket:"

> 1) Blow up a balloon and tie the end (or pinch it closed with a heavy-duty paper binder clip.)

2) Thread a straw onto 30 feet of nylon fishing line.
3) Tape the balloon to the straw, lengthwise.
4) Attach the string to opposite walls of a room.
5) Snip the tied end of the balloon with scissors (or release the binder clip) so that the balloon is propelled across the room on the string.

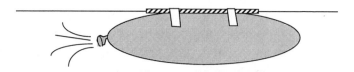

The balloon is pushed in one direction as escaping air rushes in the other direction. This is an example of Newton's second law of motion, "For every action, there is an opposite and equal reaction." Rocket ships work on the same principle, expelling burning gases instead of air.

We've spent a lot of time making our rockets go up and down different inclines, ramming two rockets from opposite directions, sending notes on the rockets, and so on. (Of course, I don't really enjoy this stuff. I just do it for the kids!)

2. Giant Straw Sculptures: Gather together a large collection of plastic drinking straws and paper clips. Open up one of the paper clips so that the two rounded corners are facing away from each other. Fit a straw over the fat end of one paper clip. Paper clip manufacturers have kindly designed their product so that you can spread the narrow end a bit, and get a snug fit on that end as well.

Your child will discover that he can make shapes (like a triangle, square, and hexagon) by fitting together a number of straws. Now for the real fun: You can join more than two straws together at any one point to form all sorts of polyhedrons and sculptures.

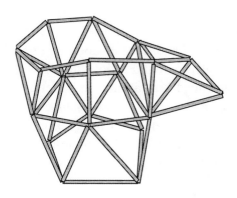

3. <u>Looking for Changes:</u> Let your child look around a room for 2 or 3 minutes, and then have him leave while you make some changes. Depending on your little detective's age and skill, you might:

Rearrange books in a bookcase
Turn on a different lamp
Interchange pictures on a wall
Move some light furniture
Crack a door open

Then call your child back in the room and let him see how many changes he can find. (Of course, you don't want to make things *too* difficult because you know what comes next. Your turn!)

For years, we've had a family tradition that is a variation on this theme. Anybody who gets his or her hands on our little stuffed toy monkey can hide him. He has shown up hanging on the milk jug in the refrigerator, diapered on the changing table, and spinning around on the record turntable with out-stretched hands.

4. <u>Meet Your Tree:</u> Our family seldom takes a nature walk without bringing a handkerchief along for this. Here's how it goes: When you have found a spot with lots of trees, blindfold your child and lead him around in different directions for awhile. Take him to a tree a short distance from your starting point (10-40 yards depending on his age), and say, "Meet your tree." The first time, help him explore the tree and become thoroughly familiar with it:

> What does it smell like?
> Is the trunk divided?
> What does the bark feel like?
> How big are the branches?
> Can you reach around the trunk?
> Are the branches alive or dead?
> How do the roots enter the ground?

Then lead your child back to the starting point, spin him around, remove the blindfold, and say, "Find your tree!" At first, it may not be easy, but you'll be amazed at how quickly children become adept at this. (Then get ready for your turn.)

5. <u>The Car Memory Game:</u> This is a good antidote for, "Are we almost there?" As you're driving along, tell everyone to take a good, close look at the car in front for about a minute. Then have them close their eyes and try to answer your toughest questions:

How many people are in the car?
How many mirrors are there?
What state is on the license plate?
What is the license plate number?
Is anyone wearing a hat?
What is on the rear window ledge?
What is in the trunk?

I save the last one for when they get over-confident. Of course, the best thing about this game is they can't play against you and show you up. You simply say, "Kids, I *know* I could beat you...but I'm driving so I can't close my eyes."

6. <u>Game of Latitude and Longitude:</u> With a globe or map containing latitude and longitude lines, show your child that any location can be described by giving first its latitude (the horizontal line or parallel) and then its longitude (the vertical line or meridian). To play this game, you'll need a world atlas or set of encyclopedias and a box divided into 6 sections as shown (or six bowls in a line):

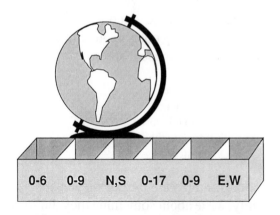

Into the first compartment on the left, put pieces of paper labeled 0, 1, 2, 3, 4, 5 and 6. Put labeled pieces into the remaining compartments as shown above.

Each person takes a turn being an astronaut whose space shuttle is going to make an emergency landing somewhere in the world. To find out where, the player draws one piece of paper from each compartment, left to right. For example, if the following pieces are drawn—1-7-S-4-5-E—the location would be latitude 17 degrees south, longitude 45 degrees east. This is Madagascar.

The player then tells what he'll find upon landing: What form of government exists? Is the land densely populated? What types of food are eaten? What religion is practiced? What is the standard of living? Do you know of someone who was born there? What products are exported? The player tells everything he knows about Madagascar—which, by the way, is a very short conversation for me. That's when an atlas or encyclopedia can be used to help. Imagine how much more your child will remember about Madagascar than if he had simply been assigned to read it in a textbook.

7. <u>Hide a Note:</u> This is one of our favorites. It encourages appreciation in the sender, gives a warm feeling to the receiver, and blends in some good laughs with a touch of mystery. Begin by writing notes to other family members and then place them in fun, unusual spots:

> Inside a shoe
> Under a plate
> Taped to a favorite toy
> Tied to a toothbrush
> On the steering wheel

In your notes, simply tell the person you are glad he or she is in the family, write about something they did for which you are grateful, give your wishes for a great day, or write whatever will give a smile, a blessing, a feeling of being loved. With very little encouragement, your children will soon be leaving notes around the house. I remember one cold dark morning as I was getting ready to go to work. I wasn't looking forward to that particular day, but as I put on one of my socks I felt something that changed my whole outlook. "Daddy," the note said, "I love you very, very much!"

Tips on Setting Up Your Activity Times

When I come home from work I don't feel creative juices pulsing through my brain. And I'm not given to outbursts of, "Hey kids, I just had a *great* idea for something we could try!" No, when I come home from work my brain has turned to mush.

If I'm going to be Mr. Wizard tonight, I must have been Mr. Preparation some other day. If you have the same problem, I'd recommend you gather creative ideas, jot them down on 5 by 8-inch index cards, and store them in a prominently displayed file box. Where do these great ideas come from? Do some hunting at your library and bookstore. Many school teacher supplies have ideas that can be spiced up for smaller groups. If you can find some old family game and activity books, you'll have a real gold-mine. (Before the advent of television, many idea books were written to support our civilization's unusual custom of spending time in family groups.) Finally, I've found that if I actually *think* from time to time, *I* can even come up with some ideas.

As you gather the ideas, you might want to ask yourself these five questions:

1) Can it be done together?
2) Will it be fun for all of us?
3) Is it educational?
4) Is little or no preparation required?
5) Can most activities be done in a single evening or a Saturday afternoon?

After you have gathered and screened these ideas, there are a few things to keep in mind before you start:

Check your attitude before beginning—You are like a mirror for your child. If you are having fun, your child will have fun!

Check your child's condition—Does your child look like he is suffering from sleep deprivation? Or is he loaded up on sugar, climbing up one wall, across the ceiling, and down the other? Better wait till tomorrow night.

Build excitement—Get them thinking about the activity to come. I like to use the phrase, "After supper wouldja like to..."

Adapt activities to meet each child's age—If you were explaining gravity to a very young child, you might get out a globe and explain that gravity pulls everything toward the center. You might let a somewhat older child closely watch the speed of an object the instant it falls from your hand, and then just before it hits the floor (to explain that gravity *accelerates* things). Or you could read of Galileo's experiment from the tower of Pisa.

Experiment—Allow enough time for everyone to ask "what if" questions. Think of each activity as a springboard for creativity and experimentation and further learning—not a cookbook recipe to rush through.

Stop while it's still fun—Don't use the UTEGO method of teaching (**U**ntil **T**heir **E**yes **G**laze **O**ver). Instead, wrap it up while they're still having fun, and they'll be ready to pick it up another evening.

Chapter 25
Home Tutoring and Schooling

The scene: A remote ranch in northern California a mile from the nearest neighbor. An 18-year-old boy named Grant Colfax is leaving home in an old battered pickup truck, headed for the east coast. He had spent almost no time in a classroom before this year. Instead, he had learned economics and biology from raising and selling goats, and geometry from building a shed. He had read a *lot* by a kerosene lamp. As he put it, "If you had a choice between splitting a cord of wood or sitting down to study three chapters of biology, you'd probably pick biology too."[1]

Where is he going? To Harvard to study biology on a full scholarship. His admission test scores had all been above ninety percentile, but more importantly, he had a *love for learning*. Robert Cashion, the Harvard admissions officer who interviewed Grant said, "the young man struck me as someone who really enjoyed the learning process. It was refreshing to see."[2]

Because Grant wanted to make sure he could adjust to formal school life, he signed up for and received straight A's in five classes at a junior college: "It was much easier than I thought it would be, although I found myself really getting bored when teachers spent a lot of time explaining why we had to read the assigned books. To me, it's perfectly obvious why you have to read classics."[3]

Grant Colfax has since graduated from Harvard with high honors and two of his younger brothers, Drew and Reed, have followed his footsteps to Harvard. These boys also learned at home by bringing electricity to the ranch with solar power, building a telescope and observatory, and so forth.

I don't relate this story to describe the typical home-schooled family. Nor is it the model for all families to emulate. Few master craftsmen, gifted musicians, or pastors have received their education at an Ivy League college. And I believe this example doesn't address the most important lessons we can teach at home—values. My point is simply that we must never think of the home as a place for a second-rate education. On the contrary, under your guidance, your child's potential for learning is enormous in this setting.

Does this mean your child must be deprived if you don't pull him out of school and begin teaching him at home? No, the benefits of home schooling during the day and home tutoring during the evenings, weekends, and summer are largely the same. There are some fundamental and compelling reasons why your child will learn better from you in the home than from a teacher in a classroom. Remember that these reasons apply *after* public or Christian school as well as in a home school.

1) Mastery Concept of Learning—In the classroom, the amount of time given to most lessons remains constant while the quality of learning varies from child to child. Sarah is bored because she understood the lesson 10 minutes ago, but Matthew is still struggling when the teacher moves on. The opposite occurs in home tutoring: The quality of learning is held constant while the amount of time required for each lesson varies. You don't move on until your child *masters* the subject.

2) Excellent Student-to-Teacher Ratio—For years schools have tried to reduce their student-to-teacher ratios so teachers can be more responsive to their students. When you are tutoring your child, you already have the optimum ratio: one-to-one! After an in-depth study of more than 1000 classrooms, John Goodlad (UCLA), found that the average teacher responded to individual students only seven minutes per day.[4] That's seven minutes per teacher—not seven minutes per student! According to Moore, "In a reasonably loving and responsive home, the average family-schooled child often receives fifty to a hundred times as many adult-to-child responses."[5]

3) Learning Through Questions—Since the days of Socrates, the use of questions has been regarded as an effective teaching technique. Yet this process suffers in the typical school as shown by a study of *wait time* by Mary Budd Rowe (University of Florida).[6] Wait time is the silent time that passes after the teacher asks a question; if an answer is not returned quickly enough, the teacher repeats, rephrases, or asks another question. For 197 out of 200 teachers monitored, the pace of instruction was "very fast," with an average wait time of only one second. When teachers were trained to increase their wait times to 3-5 seconds many benefits followed:

- Responses were longer
- Student confidence increased
- "I don't know" responses decreased
- Greater speculative thinking occurred
- More student questions arose

When you are tutoring your child at home, you have a great opportunity to slow the pace down, wait patiently for answers, and truly invigorate your child's thinking process.

4) Greater Feedback and Accountability—In the classroom, your child may not know what he doesn't know until his graded test is returned days later. In the tutoring process, you can immediately detect problem areas and help him master them.

5) Loving, Caring Instruction—Across this country there are many school teachers who have poured themselves, heart and soul, into helping their students. On the whole, however, a teacher cannot have the heart for your child that you have. And it is this love, this concern, this responsiveness you can give in your home that ultimately makes it *the* most powerful forum for learning.

The intent of these last few chapters has been to show that Mom and Dad's role in the learning process should go beyond getting their child ready in time for the school bus. You are in charge of his learning process and it's up to you to plan the curriculum of his childhood. You can do this with creative play, work education, creative learning activities, home tutoring, or home schooling. It's up to you. In so many ways, the more involved you become the more your child will benefit—and the more you'll enjoy!

Chapter 26

Numbering Our Days

Cut back on the TV. Find time to read to your children. Get involved with their peer group. Spend time having devotions, touching palates, reinforcing character, setting boundaries, building family memories. Check into the school curriculum. Get involved in your child's learning process.

Oh, boy. These are ways to reverse the trends, all right, but the costs in terms of your time and energy are tremendous. For most of us, we are talking about a very real change in *lifestyle*. What could possibly motivate you to make such a change? I don't know, but let me tell you three things that motivate me when I don't feel like getting motivated. Perhaps you'll feel the same tug that I do.

#1: It's My Duty

I don't think the word "duty" has quite the same back-straightening, chin-jutting effect on mankind that it once did. More recently, I've heard duty defined as any task we look forward to with distaste, perform with reluctance, and brag about afterwards. Yet I know that I've been given nothing more important to do in this life than the duty of rearing my children. In Psalms 127:4,5 we read:

Reversing the Trends...

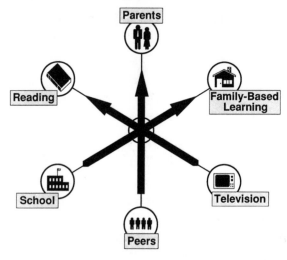

Like arrows in the hands of a warrior are sons born in one's youth.
Blessed is the man whose quiver is full of them...[1]

Imagine you are a Hebrew warrior. There are certain rules for handling arrows you need to know. The first is to know your arrows. Since each is hand-crafted, you need to study it to know how it will fly. (You won't show up for battle with questions like, "Pointy side out, right Sarge?") The second rule is to stay close to your arrows. If you leave them lying around, they might get stepped on during the battle. Or worse, as the battlefield shifts, the enemy might pick up your own arrows and aim them at you. And third, you need to carefully aim each arrow, so that it will fly straight and true to the mark.

In a day when too many parents have lost touch with their children, I need to *know my arrows*. In a day when too many families are being wounded by drugs, alcohol, and rebellion, I need to *stay close to my arrows*. And in a day when too many children lack integrity, purpose, and a reliance on God, I need to *aim my arrows*. For it is my duty.

#2: Kids Are Fun

Have you ever wondered why the same children that give Mom and Dad fits are also able to give such a thrill to Grandma and Grandpa? Do these children go through a metamorphosis after they get out of your car and just before they cross your parents' threshold? Or could it be that Grandma and Grandpa have different expectations for their time together with those little monkeys?

I've never been accused of being too bright, but this I have learned: Kids are fun! The other day, my daughters and I made a big marble racetrack using sloping curtain rods— open-end up—with funnels to transfer the marbles from rod to rod. (It takes 43 seconds for each marble to travel from our second-floor hall to the basement, in case you were wondering.) *I had a ball!* But wouldn't it have looked silly for a grown adult to do that by himself?

For the past week, we've been reading (and trying to guess the identity) of *The Scarlet Pimpernel.*[2] I wouldn't have had half the fun just reading it to myself. And so it goes—a hike in the woods, a board game, a trip to the library—children make it fun. The trick is to slow down our high-speed lives long enough for our children to brighten them up.

#3: Our Days Are Numbered

Carol and I know that our days with our children are numbered. They will only be in our home for six or seven thousand days. Then we won't have them to ourselves anymore. No little girl will come toddling toward me with outstretched arms in the "pick-me-up-Daddy" position. No one will be asking me to pump up her bicycle tire. No bright little face will ask if she can ride in the car with me as I go on a couple of errands.

Perhaps more than anything else, it is this knowledge that our time is so fleeting that motivates me. There will come a day when our house will be much quieter. On that day, I don't believe I'll wish I had spent more time fixing the window screens or staying late at the office. But I can see myself wishing for just one more day with my little girls, snuggled close to my side, as we read together. One more day to hold their hands as we walk to the donut store.

Just six or seven thousand days. Such a short time to hug our children, to laugh with our children, to love our children... Such a short time to rear our children.

End Notes

Chapter 1

1. From the true account of the British intelligence master, Sir Stephenson. William Stevenson, *A Man Called Intrepid: The Secret War* (New York, NY: Ballantine Books, 1976), pp. 235-56.
2. II Timothy 3:16, *New International Version Bible* (Grand Rapids, MI: Zondervan, 1985), p. 1846.
3. Deuteronomy 6:6,7, *ibid.*, p. 254.

Chapter 2

1. Urie Bronfenbrenner, *Two Worlds of Childhood* (New York, NY: Russell Sage Foundation, 1970), p. 95.
2. *Ibid.*, pp. 96-97.
3. Arthur Calhoun, *A Social History of the American Family from Colonial Times to Present* (New York, NY: Arno Press, 1973), p. 124.
4. Based on the percent of population aged 5-17 enrolled multiplied by the average number of days attended by each pupil enrolled. W. Vance Grant and Thomas D. Snyder, *Digest of Education Statistics, 1985-86* (Washington, DC: U.S. Government Printing Office, 1987), p. 30.
5. *Diary of Cotton Mather, Vol. I* (New York, NY: Frederick Ungar Publishing Co., 1957), pp. 534-37.
6. *Thank God I'm a Country Boy*, Words and music by John Martin Sommers (Cherry Lane Music, 1974).
7. Tom and Nancy Biracree, *Almanac of the American People* (New York, NY: Oxford Press, 1988), pp. 275-76. Total U.S. average was calculated from data which was based on a 1985 A. C. Nielsen survey.
8. *What Works, Research About Teaching and Learning* (U.S. Department of Education, 1986), p. 11.
9. Research done by Frank Stafford, et. al. at the Institute for Social Research— University of Michigan on 1500 American households in 1975. Quoted from Joshua Fischman, "The Children's Hours," *Psychology Today* (October, 1986), p. 16.

Chapter 3

1. Neil Postman, *The Disappearance of Childhood* (New York, NY: Dell Publishing Co., 1984).
2. *Ibid.*, p. 3.
3. Richard Farson, *Birthrights* (New York, NY: Macmillan, 1974), p. 27.
4. *Ibid.*, p. 77.
5. *Ibid.*, p. 135.
6. *Ibid.*, p. 43.
7. Patricia Wald, "Making Sense out of the Rights of Youth," *Journal of the Child Welfare League of America* (1976), p. 386.
8. *Ibid.*, p. 388.
9. *Statistical Abstract of the United States, 1987* (U.S. Department of Commerce, 1987), pp. 61-69; *Statistical Abstract of the United States, 1989*, p. 70.
10. *Statistical Abstract of the United States, 1989*, p. 173; *Historical Statistics of the United States—Colonial Times to 1970, Part 1* (U.S. Department of Commerce, 1976), p. 415.

Chapter 4

1. Marie Winn, *The Plug-In Drug* (New York: Viking Press, 1977), p. 234.
2. *Nielsen Report on Television* (Northbrook, IL: A.C. Nielsen Company, 1983), p. 10.
3. Harry F. Waters, "What TV Does to Kids," *Newsweek* (February 21, 1977), p. 63.
4. Michael B. Rothenberg, M.D., "Effect of Television Violence on Children and Youth," *Seeking Solutions to Violence on Children's Television* (San Francisco, 1977), p. 5. (22,000 Hours reported in a 1980 Gallup poll.)
5. *Ibid.*
6. Tom and Nancy Biracree, *op. cit.*, pp. 275-76. Total U.S. average was calculated from data which was based on a 1985 A. C. Nielsen survey.
7. Frank Mankiewicz and Joel Swerdlow, *Remote Control* (New York, NY: Times Books, 1978), p. 17.
8. *Statistical Abstract of the United States, 1989*, p. 544; *Statistical Abstract of the United States, 1987*, p. 531.
9. Dorothy McFadden, "Television Comes to Our Children," *Parents' Magazine* (January, 1949).
10. Henrietta Battle, "TV and Your Child," *Parents' Magazine* (November, 1949).
11. Jack Gould, "What Is Television Doing to Us?" *The New York Times* (June 12, 1949).
12. *Nielsen Report on Television*, *op. cit.*, p. 3.
13. *Statistical Abstract of the United States, 1989*, p. 544; *Statistical Abstract of the United States, 1987*, p. 531.
14. Tom and Nancy Biracree, *Almanac of the American People* (New York, NY: Oxford Press, 1988), p. 241.

233

Chapter 5

1. "Dear Abby" syndicated column, June 14, 1975.
2. Karl Albrecht, *Brain Power* (Englewood Cliffs, NJ: Prentice-Hall, Inc., 1980), p. 5.
3. Jerry Mander, *Four Arguments for the Elimination of Television* (New York, NY: William Morrow and Company, 1978), p. 194.
4. *Ibid.*, pp. 206-7.
5. *Ibid.*, p. 210.
6. *Ibid.*, p. 211.

Chapter 6

1. Jim Trelease, *The Read-Aloud Handbook* (New York, NY: Penguin Books, 1982), p. 93.
2. National Assessment of Educational Progress, 1984. Reported by Joyce D. Stern and Mary Frase Williams (ed.), *The Condition of Education* (U.S. Department of Education, 1986), p. 77.
3. Trelease, *op. cit.*, p. 95.
4. E. B. White quoted in "Why Johnny Can't Write," *Newsweek* (December 8, 1975).
5. *Statistical Abstract of the United States, 1989*, pp. 144, 544; *Statistical Abstract of the United States, 1987*, pp. 135, 531.
6. Mander, *op. cit.*, p. 308.
7. *Ibid.*
8. *Ibid.*, p. 310.
9. Gerald Lesser, *Children and Television* (New York, NY: Random House, 1974).
10. Winn, *op. cit.*, p. 38.
11. Paul Copperman, *The Literacy Hoax* (New York, NY: William Morrow and Co., 1978), pp. 58, 59.
12. Mankiewicz and Swerdlow, *op. cit.*, p. 177.
13. Norman Morris, *Television's Child* (Boston: Brown Publishing Co., 1971).
14. Albrecht, *op. cit.*, p. 6.
15. *Ibid.*, p. 5.
16. 11:00 pm news, CBS, Cleveland, Ohio, August 2, 1989.
17. Jerome and Dorothy Singer, "A Member of the Family," *Yale Alumni Magazine* (March, 1975).
18. Winn, *op. cit.*, p. 88.
19. U.S. Surgeon General, *Report on Television and Social Behavior* (1972).
20. Mander, *op. cit.*, p. 255.
21. Winn, *op. cit.*, p. 78.
22. *Ibid.*, p. 80.
23. Rothenberg, *op. cit.*, p. 5.
24. David Elkind, *The Hurried Child: Growing Up Too Fast Too Soon* (Reading, MA: Addison-Wesley, 1982), p. 78.
25. Mankiewicz and Swerdlow, *op. cit.*, p. 241.
26. Winn, *op. cit.*, p. 199.

234

27. *Health Scene*, Spring, 1986.
28. Trelease, *op. cit.*, p. 97.
29. Carl M. Cannon, "Mass of Evidence Shows TV Violence Harmful," *Akron Beacon Journal* (June 4, 1989), p. D1.
30. *Ibid.*
31. *Ibid.*
32. *Ibid.*
33. *Ibid.*
34. Mankiewicz and Swerdlow, *op. cit.*, p. 7.
35. Kevin Perrota, "Watching While Life Goes By," *Christianity Today* (April 18, 1980), p. 18.
36. Philippians 4:8, *NIV Study Bible*, p. 1809.
37. C. S. Lewis, *The Screwtape Letters* (Westwood, NJ: Barbour & Co., 1961), p. 65.
38. Vidal Sasoon on his own talk show as quoted by Neil Postman, *Disappearance of Childhood*, p. 81.
39. *Nielsen Report on Television*, *op. cit.*, p. 16.
40. Mankiewicz and Swerdlow, *op. cit.*, p. 26.
41. Jung Bay Ra, "A Comparison of Preschool Children's Preferences for Television and Their Parents," *The Journal of Social Psychology*, Vol. 102 (1977), pp. 163-64.
42. Copperman, *op. cit.*, p. 166.
43. F. Thomas Juster and Frank P. Stafford, *Time, Goods, and Well-Being* (University of Michigan, 1985), p. 368.

Chapter 7

1. Norah Davies quoted in *Better Homes and Gardens* (July, 1988).

Chapter 8

1. Trelease, *op. cit.*, p. 11.
2. "60 Million Adults Reported Illiterate," *Akron Beacon Journal* (August 4, 1985).
3. *Ibid.*
4. *What Works, Research About Teaching and Learning*, (U.S. Department of Education, 1986), p. 11.
5. Copperman, *op. cit.*, p. 99.
6. *Ibid.*
7. *Ibid.*
8. Trelease, *op. cit.*, p. 25.
9. *Ibid.*, p. 95.
10. Rudyard Kipling, *The Jungle Book* (New York, NY: Grosset & Dunlap, 1893), p. 190.

Chapter 9

1. Joshua Hammer, "The Education of Robert Allen," *People Weekly* (September 17, 1984), p. 34.
2. U.S. Department of Education, *Becoming a Nation of Readers: What Parents Can Do* (Lexington, MA: D.C. Heath and Co., 1985).
3. *What Works, op. cit.*, p. 9.
4. Trelease, *op. cit.*, p. 28.
5. *Ibid.*, p. 11.
6. Letter to Ann Landers column, "Grand Testimonial for Good Books," *Akron Beacon Journal* (June 7, 1988.)
7. Chester E. Finn, Jr., Assistant Education Secretary, quoted in "Parents Can Help Children Learn to Read," *Akron Beacon Journal* (1985).
8. *What Works, op. cit.*, p. 21.
9. Samuel L. Blumenfeld, *How to Tutor* (Milford, MI: Mott Media, 1973).
10. Victor and Mildred Goertzel, *Cradles of Eminence* (Boston, MA: Little, Brown & Co., 1962), p. 7.
11. Susan Schaeffer Macaulay, *For the Children's Sake* (Westchester, IL: Crossway Books, 1984), p. 15.
12. Trelease, *op. cit.*, p. 112.
13. C. S. Lewis, "On Three Ways of Writing for Children," *The Horn Book* (October 1963), pp. 459-69.
14. Trelease, *op. cit.* p. 109.
15. *What Works, op. cit.*, p. 11.

Chapter 10

1. Frank B. Gilbreth, Jr. and Ernestine Gilbreth Carey, *Cheaper by the Dozen* (Garden City, NY: International Collectors Library, 1948), pp. 11-14.

Chapter 11

1. *Webster's New World Dictionary of the American Language, Second College Edition* (New York, NY: World Publishing, 1972), p. 1351.
2. Romans 12:2, *The Scofield Reference Bible, King James Version* (New York, NY: Oxford Press, 1945), p. 1206.
3. Proverbs 22:15, *NIV Study Bible* (Grand Rapids, MI: The Zondervan Corporation, 1985), p. 977.
4. Proverbs 13:20, *ibid.*, p. 964.
5. Bronfenbrenner, *op. cit.*, p. 96.

Chapter 12

1. Phrase coined by Urie Bronfenbrenner, referenced by Raymond and Dorothy Moore, *Home-Spun Schools* (Waco, TX: Word Books, 1982), pp. 9-10.
2. James Dobson, quoted in "Socialization," *The Teaching Home* (August/ September, 1984), p. 11.

3. Bronfenbrenner, *op. cit.*, pp. 117-18.
4. Dale Farran, "Now For the Bad News," *Parents* (September, 1982), p. 81.
5. I Kings 12:6-8, *The NIV Study Bible,* p. 496.
6. Goertzel, *op. cit.*, p. 269.

Chapter 13

1. W. Vance Grant and Thomas D. Snyder, *Digest of Education Statistics, 1985-86* (Washington, DC: U.S. Government Printing Office, 1987), p. 30.
2. Farran, *op. cit.*, p. 81.
3. Robert G. Andry, *Delinquency and Parental Pathology* (London: Methuen & Co., Ltd, 1960), p. 45.
4. Bronfenbrenner, *op. cit.*, pp. 101-2.
5. *Ibid.*
6. Joan E. Grusec and Rona Abramovitch (University of Toronto), "Imitation of Peers and Adults in a Natural Setting: A Functional Analysis," *Child Development,* Vol. 53, No. 3 (June, 1982), p. 640.
7. Hans Sebald (Arizona State University), "Adolescents' Shifting Orientation toward Parents and Peers: A Curvilinear Trend over Recent Decades," *Journal of Marriage and the Family,* Vol. 48 (February, 1986), pp. 10-11.

Chapter 14

1. Zig Ziglar, *See You At The Top* (Gretna, LA: Pelican Publishing Co., 1975), p. 148.
2. Jung Bay Ra, op. cit., pp. 163-64.
3. Robert S. Welch, "Making Your Family Number One in '87," *Focus on the Family* (January, 1987), p. 4.
4. *Historical Statistics of the U.S., Colonial Times to 1970* (U.S. Dept. of Commerce, 1976) Series D 63-74; *Statistical Abstract of the U.S., 1989* (U.S. Dept. of Commerce, 1989) p. 386.
5. James Dobson, *Hide or Seek* (Old Tappan, NJ: Fleming H. Revell Co., 1974), p. 64.

Chapter 15

1. Harold M. Skeels, "Adult Status of Children with Contrasting Early Life Experiences," *Monographs of the Society for Research in Child Development,* Vol. 31 (1966), Serial No. 105.
2. Bronfenbrenner, *op. cit.*, p. 141.
3. *Ibid.*, p. 140.
4. Marcelle Geber, "The Psycho-Motor Development of African Children in the First Year, and the Influence of Maternal Behavior," *The Journal of Social Psychology,* Vol. 47 (1958), pp. 185-195.
5. *Ibid.*, p. 194.
6. Richard Restak, *The Brain: The Last Frontier* (Garden City, NY: Doubleday & Co., 1979), p. 123.

7. *Ibid.*, p. 122.
8. "After 10-Year Day-Care Study, Psychologist Changes His Stance," *Focus on the Family* (August, 1987), p. 10.
9. Karl Zinsmeister, "Is Infant Day Care Ruining Our Kids?" *Focus on the Family Citizen* (February, 1989), p. 6.
10. Ken Magid and Carole A. McKelvey, *High Risk* (New York, NY: Bantam Books, 1987).
11. Thomas J. Gamble and Edward Zigler, "Effects of Infant Day Care: Another Look at the Evidence," *American Journal of Orthopsychiatry*, Vol. 56 (January, 1986), p. 35.
12. *Ibid.*, p. 26.
13. Andry, *op. cit.*, p. 46.
14. Linda Thompson, Alan C. Acock and Kelvin Clark, "Do Parents Know Their Children? The Ability of Mothers and Fathers to Gauge the Attitudes of Their Young Adult Children," *Family Relations*, Vol. 34 (July, 1985), pp. 315-20.
15. Jean Fleming, *A Mother's Heart* (Colorado Springs, CO: NavPress, 1982), p. 114.
16. *Ibid.*
17. Thomas W. Miller, "Paternal Absence and its Effect on Adolescent Self-Esteem," *The International Journal of Social Psychiatry*, Vol. 30, No. 4 (Winter, 1984), pp. 293-96.
18. A. Barclay and D. R. Cusumano, "Father Absence, Cross-Sex Identity, and Field Dependent Behavior in Male Adolescents," *Child Development*, Vol. 38 (1967), pp. 243-50.
19. George R. Bach, "Father-Fantasies and Father-Typing in Father-Separated Children," *Child Development*, Vol. 17 (1946), pp. 63-79.
20. David B. Lynn and William L. Sawyer, "The Effects of Father-Absence on Norwegian Boys and Girls," *Journal of Abnormal and Social Psychology*, Vol. 59 (1959), pp. 258-62.
21. Walter Mischel, "Father-Absence and Delay of Gratification: Cross-cultural Comparison," *Journal of Abnormal and Social Psychology*, Vol. 63 (1961), pp. 116-24.

Chapter 16

1. Proverbs 22:6, *King James Version Bible,* pp. 687-88.
2. Charles R. Swindoll, *You and Your Child* (Nashville, Tennessee: Thomas Nelson Inc., 1977), p. 19.
3. Gregg Harris, *The Christian Home School* (Brentwood, Tennessee: Wolgemuth & Hyatt, 1988), p. 64.
4. Portion of Proverbs 4:8,9, *NIV Study Bible*, p. 951.
5. Portion of Proverbs 17:25, *ibid.*, p. 970.
6. Dobson, Hide or Seek, *op. cit.*, p. 81.
7. Portion of Proverbs 16:32, *King James Version Bible,* p. 684.
8. Portion of Luke 16:10, *NIV Study Bible*, p. 1572.
9. "Training Grounds" is a term used by Gregg Harris in his "Home Schooling Workshop."
10. James Dobson, *Dare to Discipline* (Wheaton, IL: Tyndale House, 1970).
11. Dobson, *Hide or Seek, op. cit.*, pp. 92-93.
12. I Peter 4:8, *NIV Study Bible*, p. 1894.
13. David Mains, *50 Days to Open My Home to Christ* (Wheaton, IL: The Chapel of the Air, 1986).

14. "Flash-a-Cards" are sets of 10" by 13" full-color Bible scene illustrations that are supplied with a narrative. A Beka Book Publications, Box 18000, Pensacola, Florida 32523.

15. Kenneth W. Osbeck, *101 Hymn Stories* (Grand Rapids, MI: Kregel Publications, 1982).

Chapter 17

1. Edward Plass, *What Luther Says: A Practical-in-Home Anthology for the Active Christian* (St. Louis: Concordia, 1987), p. 449.

2. Samuel L. Blumenfeld, *NEA: Trojan Horse in American Education* (Boise, ID: The Paradigm Co., 1984), p. 3.

3. John W. Whitehead, *Parents' Rights* (Westchester, IL: Crossway Books, 1985), p. 65.

4. *Ibid.*, p. 78.

5. *Ibid.*

6. Blumenfeld, *op. cit.*, p. 2.

7. *Ibid.*, p. 8.

8. *Ibid.*, p. 9.

9. *Ibid.*, p. 15.

10. *Ibid.*, pp. 16-17.

11. *Ibid.*, p. 96.

12. *Ibid.*, p. 97.

13. *Ibid.*

14. Diane Ravitch, *The Great School Wars: New York City 1805-1973* (New York, NY: Basic Books, Inc., 1974), p. 37.

15. *Common School Journal*, Vol. 11, No. 14 (July 15, 1849), pp. 212-13.

16. Blumenfeld, *op. cit.*, p. 29.

17. *Ibid.*, p. 48.

18. *Ibid.*, p. 37.

19. W. Vance Grant and Thomas D. Snyder, *op. cit.*, p. 30.

20. John Dewey, *The School and Society* (Chicago: 1899), p. 19.

21. John Dewey, *Liberalism and Social Action* (New York, NY: G. P. Putnam's Sons, 1935), p. 52.

22. G. Stanley Hall, *Educational Problems* (New York, NY: 1911), pp. 443-44.

23. Blumenfeld, *op. cit.*, p. 100.

24. *Ibid.*

25. *School and Society*, Vol. 1, No. 5 (January 30, 1915), p. 179.

26. Blumenfeld, *op. cit.*, pp. 58-62.

27. *Humanist Manifesto I & II* (Buffalo, NY: Prometheus Books, 1973), p. 7.

28. Blumenfeld, *op. cit.*, pp. 113, 114.

29. Rudolph Flesch, *Why Johnny Can't Read* (New York, NY: Harper & Brothers, 1955), p. 5.

30. Blumenfeld, *op. cit.*, p. 120.

31. *Humanist Manifesto I & II*, *op. cit.*

32. Phyllis Schlafly (ed.), *Child Abuse in the Classroom* (Alton, IL: Pere Marquette Press, 1984), p. 15.

33. *Ibid.*, p. 155.

34. Beatrice and Ronald Gross (ed.), "A Nation at Risk," *The Great School Debate* (New York, NY: Simon & Schuster, 1985), p. 23.
35. Phyllis Schlafly, *op. cit.*, p. 18.
36. *Ibid.*

Chapter 18

1. *The Humanist* (January/February, 1976).
2. John J. Dumphy, *The Humanist* (January/February, 1983), p. 26.
3. Steve Neptune, *Akron Beacon Journal* (April 10, 1984).
4. Mel and Norma Gabler, *What Are They Teaching Our Kids?* (Wheaton, IL: SP Publications, 1986), p. 119.
5. Tim LaHaye, *The Battle for the Public Schools* (Old Tappan, NJ: Fleming H. Revell Co., 1983), p. 31.
6. Gablers, *op. cit.*, p. 129.
7. *Ibid.*, pp. 118-19.
8. Schlafly, *op. cit.*, pp. 65-66.
9. *Ibid.*, p. 366.
10. *Ibid.*, p. 261.
11. *Ibid.*, p. 57.
12. *Ibid.*, p. 102.
13. *Ibid.*, p. 244.
14. *Ibid.*, p. 126.
15. *Ibid.,* p. 265.
16. *Ibid.*, p. 64.
17. Ephesians 6:1, *NIV Study Bible*, p. 1799.
18. Schlafly, *op. cit.*, p. 57.
19. *Ibid.*
20. Leviticus 19:11, *King James Version Bible*, p. 151.
21. Paul Blanchard, "Three Cheers for Our Secular State," *The Humanist* (March/April, 1976), p. 17.
22. *Ibid.*
23. *Psychology for You* (Oxford Book Co., 1973), p. 191.
24. *Many Peoples, One Nation* (Random House, Inc., 1973), p. 88.
25. *A Global History of Man* (Allyn & Bacon, Inc., 1970), p. 444.
26. Gablers, *op. cit.*, p. 48.
27. *Ibid.*, p. 47.
28. *NEA Bicentennial Ideabook*, cited in *The Freemen Digest* (September, 1978), p. 65.
29. Schlafly, *op. cit.*, p. 230.
30. *Ibid.*
31. *Ibid.*
32. *Modern Health, Teacher's Edition* (Holt, Rinehart and Winston, 1980), p. T40.
33. *Ibid.*
34. *Sex Information and Educational Council of the United States, Position Statement 1974* as cited in LITE (Let's Improve Today's Education) Newsletter, No 69 (May, 1979), p. 563.

35. LaHaye, *op. cit.*, p. 117.
36. Gary Allen, "Sex Study," *American Opinion*, Vol. 12 (March, 1969), p. 3.
37. Schlafly, *op. cit.*, p. 110.
38. *Masculinity and Femininity, Instructor's Guide* (Houghton Mifflin Co., 1971), p. 14.
39. *Biology* (Saunders College Publishing, 1982), pp. 578-79.
40. Schlafly, *op. cit.*, p. 42.
41. Schlafly, *op. cit.*, p. 148.
42. George Grant, "Grand Illusions: The Legacy of Planned Parenthood," *Concerned Women of America* (June, 1988), p. 4.
43. Rebecca Hagelin, "Mothers Protest Sex Education in Texas Schools," *Concerned Women of America* (June, 1988), pp. 12-16.
44. Gablers, *op. cit.*, p. 92.
45. Portion of Phil. 4:8, *NIV Study Bible*, p. 1809.
46. *Messageways on a Small Planet* (Cassell Australia Ltd., 1974), p. 135.
47. "Death Education—Emotional Manipulation," in Mel and Norma Gabler, *Death Education: Handbook No. 8* (Longview, TX: Educational Research Analysts, 1981), p. 2.
48. LaHaye, *The Battle for the Public Schools, op. cit.*, p. 208.
49. Mel and Norma Gabler, *Death Education: Handbook No. 8* (Longview, TX: Educational Research Analysts, 1981), p. 2.
50. Schlafly, *op. cit.*, p. 262.
51. *Ibid.*, p. 308.
52. Gabler, *op. cit.*, p. 19; Schlafly, *op. cit.*, p. 262.
53. Gary Allen, "Problems, Propaganda, and Pornography," *American Opinion*, Vol. 12 (March, 1969), p. 12.
54. Private research conducted by Cullen Davis, P.O. Box 1224, Ft. Worth, TX 76101, cited by Gablers.
55. Schlafly, *op. cit.*, p. 124.

Chapter 19

1. Dick Feagler, The "Unawakened", *Akron Beacon Journal* (Nov. 12, 1986).
2. Copperman, *op. cit.*, p. 37.
3. *Statistical Abstract of the U. S., 1989*, p. 144; Copperman, *op. cit.*, p. 38.
4. Copperman, *op. cit.*, p. 40.
5. *Ibid.*, p. 38.
6. *Ibid.*, p. 42.
7. Beatrice and Ronald Gross (ed.), "A Nation at Risk," *The Great School Debate* (New York, NY: Simon & Schuster, Inc., 1985), p. 26.
8. Copperman, *op. cit.*, p. 79.
9. *Ibid.*, p. 81.
10. *Ibid.*, p. 104.
11. *Ibid.*, p. 105.
12. *Ibid.*
13. William H. Miller, "Employers Wrestle with 'Dumb Kids,'" *Industry Week* (July 4, 1988), p. 47.
14. David T. Kearns, quoted in Los Angeles article, reported in *Christian School Comment*, Vol 18, No. 4.
15. Stern and Williams, *op. cit.*, p. 48.
16. *Ibid.*

17. Copperman, *op. cit.*, p. 135.
18. *Ibid.*, p. 143.
19. "A Nation at Risk", *op. cit.*, p. 26.
20. "The Condition of Education," *op. cit.*, p. 34.
21. Dick Feagler, "What Adds Up," *Akron Beacon Journal*.
22. Copperman, *op. cit.*, p. 47.
23. *Ibid.*
24. "Geography: A 'Survival Skill,'" *USA Today* (May 18, 1989), p. 2A.
25. E. D. Hirsch, Jr., *Cultural Literacy* (Boston, MA: Houghton Mifflin Co., 1987), p. 9.
26. *What Works, op. cit.*, p. 53.
27. Hirsch, *op. cit.*, p. 8.
28. *Ibid.*
29. "National Geographic Gives Education Grant," *Akron Beacon Journal* (January 14, 1988), p. A13.
30. Hirsch, *op. cit.*, p. XV.
31. William H. Bell, "What Farm Kids Knew in 1911," *Wall Street Journal* (July 25, 1983), cited by Gablers.
32. Results of 1982 National Assessment of Educational Progress testing, quoted in "Are Your Kids Learning to Think?" *Changing Times* (Dec., 1983).

Chapter 20

1. Portion of Luke 6:40, *NIV Study Bible,* p. 1550.
2. Portion of Hebrews 13:9, *NIV Study Bible,* p. 1876.
3. *ACSI Directory*, 1987.
4. Gabler, *op. cit.*, p. 180.
5. *Ibid.*
6. Beatrice and Ronald Gross (ed), Phil Keisling, "Do Private Schools Do It Better and Cheaper?" *The Great School Debate* (New York, NY: Simon & Schuster, 1985), p. 458.
7. Bill Ihde, "Home Schools: The Kitchen as Classroom," *The Teaching Home* (May/June 1989), p. 23.
8. John Lofton, "Godzilla Did His Homework," *The Washington Times* (September 9, 1988), p. F3.
9. Ihde, *op. cit.*, p. 23.
10. Forester, J. J., "At What Age Should a Child Start School?" *School Executive*, Vol. 74 (1955), pp. 80-81.
11. Raymond and Dorothy Moore, *Home Style Teaching* (Waco, TX: Word Books, 1984).
12. Raymond and Dorothy Moore, *Home-Spun Schools* (Waco, TX: Word Books, 1982).
13. Christian Life Workshops, P.O. Box 3456, Portland, OR 97208.
14. H. Wayne House (Ed.), *Schooling Choices* (Portland, OR: Multnomah Press, 1988).

Chapter 22

1. Macaulay, *op. cit.*, p. 21.
2. Allen W. Gottfried, "The Relationship of Play Materials and Parental In-

volvement to Young Children's Development," *Play Interactions* (Johnson & Johnson Baby Products, 1985), p. 185.
3. *Ibid.*
4. Marlene D. Fever, *Growing Creative Children* (Wheaton IL: Tyndale House Publishers, 1981), p. 68. Cites Lowenfeld and Brittain, *Creative and Mental Growth*: "It has been revealed by experimentation and research that more than half of all children exposed to coloring books lose their creativeness and their independence of expression and become rigid and dependent."
5. Macaulay, *op. cit.*, p. 85.
6. Theodore D. Wachs, "Home Stimulation and Cognitive Development," *Play Interactions* (Johnson & Johnson Baby Products, 1985), p. 143.

Chapter 23

1. Ziglar, *op. cit.*, p. 317.
2. *Ibid.*, pp. 314-15.
3. Lamentations 3:27, *NIV Study Bible*, p 1222.
4. Proverbs 22:29, *ibid.*, p. 977.

Chapter 24

1. Karl Albrecht, *op. cit.*, p. V.
2. *Ibid.*, pp. 38-44.
3. V. J. Papanek., "Solving Problems Creatively," *Management Views*, Vol. 9, No. 3 (1964), pp. 169-96.

Chapter 25

1. Eileen Garred, "The Home-Schooling Alternative," *USAir* (September, 1985), p. 10.
2. Terri Minsky, "Home-Taught Backwoods Boy Accepted to Enter Harvard," *The Boston Globe* (August 30, 1983).
3. *Ibid.*
4. John I. Goodlad, "A Study of Schooling: Some Findings and Hypotheses," *Phi Delta Kappan* (March, 1983), p. 467.
5. Raymond and Dorothy Moore, *Home Style Teaching* (Waco, TX: Word Books, 1984) p. 29.
6. Mary Budd Rowe, "Wait-Time and Rewards as Instructional Variables, Their Influence on Language, Logic, and Fate Control: Part One—Wait-Time," *Journal of Research in Science Teaching*, Vol. 11, No. 2 (1974), pp. 81-94.

Chapter 26

1. Psalm 127:4-5b, *NIV Study Bible*, p. 925.
2. Baroness Orczy, *The Scarlet Pimpernel* (Garden City, NY: International Collectors Library).

Select Bibliography

Albrecht, Karl. *Brain Power.* Englewood Cliffs, NJ: Prentice-Hall, 1980.

Andry, Robert G. *Delinquency and Parental Pathology.* London: Methuen & Co., Ltd, 1960.

Becoming a Nation of Readers: What Parents Can Do. Lexington, MA: D.C. Heath and Co., 1985.

Biracree, Tom and Nancy. *Almanac of the American People.* New York, NY: Oxford Press, 1988.

Blumenfeld, Samuel L. *How to Tutor.* Milford, MI: Mott Media, 1973.

———. *NEA: Trojan Horse in American Education.* Boise, ID: The Paradigm Co., 1984.

Bronfenbrenner, Urie. *Two Worlds of Childhood.* New York, NY: Russell Sage Foundation, 1970.

Calhoun, Arthur. *A Social History of the American Family from Colonial Times to Present.* New York, NY: Arno Press, 1973.

Cannon, Carl M. "Mass of Evidence Shows TV Violence Harmful." *Akron Beacon Journal.* June 4, 1989.

Colfax, David and Micki. *Homeschooling for Excellence.* New York, NY: Warner Books, 1988.

Copperman, Paul. *The Literacy Hoax.* New York, NY: William Morrow and Company, 1978.

Diary of Cotton Mather, Volume I. New York, NY: Frederick Ungar Publishing, 1957.

Dobson, James. *Dare to Discipline.* Wheaton, IL: Tyndale House, 1970.

———. *Hide or Seek.* Old Tappan, NJ: Fleming H. Revell, 1974.

———. Quoted in "Socialization." *The Teaching Home.* August/September, 1984.

Elkind, David. *The Hurried Child: Growing Up Too Fast Too Soon.* Reading, MA: Addison-Wesley, 1982.

Farran, Dale. "Now For the Bad News." *Parents.* September, 1982.

Farson, Richard. *Birthrights.* New York, NY: Macmillan, 1974.

Fever, Marlene D. *Growing Creative Children.* Wheaton, IL: Tyndale House Publishers, 1981.

Fleming, Jean. *A Mother's Heart.* Colorado Springs, CO: NavPress, 1982.

Flesch, Rudolph. *Why Johnny Can't Read.* New York, NY: Harper & Brothers, 1955.

Forester, J. J. "At What Age Should a Child Start School?" *School Executive.* 74:80-81, 1955.

244

Gabler, Mel and Norma. *What Are They Teaching Our Kids?* Wheaton, IL: SP Publications, 1986.

Gamble, Thomas J. and Edward Zigler. "Effects of Infant Day Care: Another Look at the Evidence." *American Journal of Orthopsychiatry.* 56:35, January, 1986.

Geber, Marcelle. "The Psycho-Motor Development of African Children in the First Year, and the Influence of Maternal Behavior." *The Journal of Social Psychology.* 47:185-95, 1958.

Goertzel, Victor and Mildred. *Cradles of Eminence.* Boston, MA: Little, Brown and Co., 1962.

Goodlad, John I. "A Study of Schooling: Some Findings and Hypotheses." *Phi Delta Kappan.* March, 1983.

Gottfried, Allen W. "The Relationship of Play Materials and Parental Involvement to Young Children's Development." *Play Interactions.* Johnson & Johnson Baby Products, 1985.

Grant, George. *Grand Illusions: The Legacy of Planned Parenthood.* Brentwood, TN: Wolgemuth & Hyatt, 1988.

Grant, W. Vance and Thomas D. Snyder. *Digest of Education Statistics, 1985-86.* Washington, DC: U.S. Government Printing Office, 1987.

Gross, Beatrice and Ronald (ed). "A Nation at Risk." *The Great School Debate.* New York, NY: Simon & Schuster, 1985.

Grusec, Joan E. and Rona Abramovitch. "Imitation of Peers and Adults in a Natural Setting: A Functional Analysis." *Child Development.* 53:640, June, 1982.

Hammer, Joshua. "The Education of Robert Allen." *People Weekly.* September 17, 1984.

Harris, Gregg. *The Christian Home School.* Brentwood, TN: Wolgemuth & Hyatt, 1988.

Hirsch, E. D., Jr. *Cultural Literacy.* Boston, MA: Houghton Mifflin Co., 1987.

Historical Statistics of the U.S., Colonial Times to 1970. U.S. Department of Commerce, 1976.

House, Wayne H. (ed). *Schooling Choices.* Portland, OR: Multnomah Press, 1988.

Humanist Manifesto I & II. Buffalo, NY: Prometheus Books, 1973.

Hunt, Gladys. *Honey for a Child's Heart.* Grand Rapids, MI: Zondervan Books, 1969.

Ihde, Bill. "Home Schools: The Kitchen as Classroom." *The Teaching Home.* May/ June, 1989.

Juster, F. Thomas and Frank P. Stafford. *Time, Goods, and Well-Being.* University of Michigan, 1985.

LaHaye, Tim. *The Battle for the Family.* Old Tappan, NJ: Fleming H. Revell Co., 1982.

———. *The Battle for the Public Schools.* Old Tappan, NJ: Fleming H. Revell Co., 1983.

Macaulay, Susan Schaeffer. *For the Children's Sake.* Westchester, IL: Crossway Books, 1984.

Magid, Ken and Carole A. McKelvey. *High Risk.* New York, NY: Bantam Books, 1987.

Mains, David. *50 Days to Open My Home to Christ.* Wheaton, IL: The Chapel of the Air, 1986.

Mander, Jerry. *Four Arguments for the Elimination of Television*. New York, NY: William Morrow and Company, 1978.

Mankiewicz, Frank and Joel Swerdlow. *Remote Control*. New York, NY: Times Books, 1978.

Meier, Paul D. *Christian Child-Rearing and Personality Development*. Grand Rapids, MI: Baker Book House, 1977.

Miller, Thomas W. "Paternal Absence and its Effect on Adolescent Self-Esteem." *The International Journal of Social Psychiatry*. 30:293-96, Winter, 1984.

Miller, William H. "Employers Wrestle with 'Dumb Kids.'" *Industry Week*. July 4, 1988.

Moore, Raymond and Dorothy. *Home-Spun Schools*. Waco, TX: Word Books, 1982.

——. *Home Style Teaching*. Waco, TX: Word Books, 1984.

New International Version Study Bible. Grand Rapids, MI: Zondervan, 1985.

Nielsen Report on Television. Northbrook, IL: A.C. Nielsen Co., 1983.

Osbeck, Kenneth W. *101 Hymn Stories*. Grand Rapids, MI: Kregel Publications, 1982.

Papanek, V. J. "Solving Problems Creatively." *Management Views*. 9:169-96, 1964.

Perrota, Kevin. "Watching While Life Goes By." *Christianity Today*. April 18, 1980.

Plass, Edward. *What Luther Says: A Practical-in-Home Anthology for the Active Christian*. St. Louis, MO: Concordia, 1987.

Postman, Neil. *The Disappearance of Childhood*. New York, NY: Dell Publishing, 1984.

Ra, Jung Bay. "A Comparison of Preschool Children's Preferences for Television and Their Parents." *The Journal of Social Psychology*. 102:163-64, 1977.

Restak, Richard. *The Brain: The Last Frontier*. Garden City, NY: Doubleday & Co., 1979.

Rothenberg, Michael B. "Effect of Television Violence on Children and Youth." *Seeking Solutions to Violence on Children's Television*. San Francisco, CA, 1977.

Rowe, Mary Budd. "Wait-Time and Rewards as Instructional Variables, Their Influence on Language, Logic, and Fate Control: Part One—Wait-Time." *Journal of Research in Science Teaching*. 11:81-94, 1974.

Schlafly, Phyllis (ed). *Child Abuse in the Classroom*. Alton, IL: Pere Marquette Press, 1984.

Sebald, Hans. "Adolescents' Shifting Orientation toward Parents and Peers: a Curvilinear Trend over Recent Decades." *Journal of Marriage and the Family*. 48:10-11, February, 1986.

Skeels, Harold M. "Adult Status of Children with Contrasting Early Life Experiences." *Monographs of the Society for Research in Child Development*. 31:105, 1966.

Statistical Abstract of the United States, 1989. U.S. Department of Commerce, 1989.

Stern, Joyce D. and Mary Frase Williams. *The Condition of Education*. U.S. Department of Education, 1986.

Swindoll, Charles R. *You and Your Child*. Nashville, TN: Thomas Nelson., 1977.

246

Thompson, Linda, Alan C. Acock, and Kelvin Clark. "Do Parents Know Their Children? The Ability of Mothers and Fathers to Gauge the Attitudes of Their Young Adult Children." *Family Relations.* 34:315-20, July, 1985.

Trelease, Jim. *The Read-Aloud Handbook.* New York, NY: Penguin Books, 1982.

Wachs, Theodore D. "Home Stimulation and Cognitive Development." *Play Interactions.* Johnson & Johnson Baby Products, 1985.

Welch, Robert S. "Making Your Family Number One in '87." *Focus on the Family.* January, 1987.

What Works, Research About Teaching and Learning. U.S. Department of Education, 1986.

Whitehead, John W. *Parents' Rights.* Westchester, IL: Crossway Books, 1985.

Wilson, Elizabeth. *Books Children Love.* Westchester, IL: Crossway Books, 1987.

Winn, Marie. *The Plug-In Drug.* New York: Viking Press, 1977.

Ziglar, Zig. *See You at the Top.* Gretna, LA: Pelican Publishing Co, 1975.

Zinsmeister, Karl. "Is Infant Day Care Ruining Our Kids?" *Focus on the Family Citizen.* February, 1989.